A STROKE OF MISFORTUNE

John Greenridge

authorHOUSE®

AuthorHouse™ UK Ltd.
500 Avebury Boulevard
Central Milton Keynes, MK9 2BE
www.authorhouse.co.uk
Phone: 08001974150

First published by AuthorHouse   09/30/2010

ISBN: 978-1-4520-5336-3

Note: All illustrations by the Author.

Dedication:

This book is dedicated to Margaret, my wife – who is the subject of what happens to be a true story.

All the characters in this story have been given fictitious identities, but those identities do represent real people and the events depicted did all happen.

Thus Mrs 'Ogl-vie' is truly an optician as is Mr Sewell (see well), while Margaret's consultant – 'Dr Geriant Olds' is a consultant Geriatrician dealing with older people!

I am ever grateful to our many friends and acquaintances who freely gave their help and support throughout Margaret's recovery. Without that help, I guess the task of aiding that recovery would have been beyond my capabilities. Thus the lack of any Social Services help or minimal NHS post-hospital support might have been more telling.

John Greenridge. 2010.

Forward

None of us knows how or when the little things we do and learn in our lifetime are going to come in useful. None of us can anticipate the moment when our lives will be dramatically altered forever by events beyond our control. Though, undoubtedly, sadly and unfortunately, many of us will experience just such an occasion within the span of our lifetime.

It may be comforting to believe that our God will prepare us for what is to come in the future, even if perhaps, this turns out not to be the case. I am presently acutely aware that some of the happenings in my life proved to have equipped me with the skills to cope with disaster when it befell my wife.

Not everyone is so fortunate in his or her Carer - as a visit to any Stroke Unit or residential care establishment may show you. Even so, when the savage blow came, it did so with a destructive force that would change the lives of both my wife and myself for the rest of our time on Earth.

Margaret's subsequent recovery to her present state of health is as good as any miracle and ably demonstrates the phenomenon of the mythical Phoenix rising from the ashes that are so symbolic of its destruction.

In this story, I have tried to relate events in the order that they occurred and to illustrate a few of those special things that prepared me to cope with the disaster when it struck down my wife, Margaret.

'Why Margaret?' I have often wondered. Why someone who was so special in her own right and so involved with life and with people in so many personal ways. She was and is again – thankfully today - such a wonderful Christian person, well loved by all who come into contact with her.

This is my story, but Margaret is the subject of it. Despite my best efforts, the dialogue cannot truly portray the raw courage displayed by my wife during her recovery. Nor can it adequately describe the powerful human force that characterised her ultimate determination to get back a fair slice of her life as she became aware of whom she had been prior to the accident.

For this most amazing recovery to take place, she would need the dedicated help and encouragement of her husband coupled to that of her many and diversely talented loyal friends.

JG 2010.

About the book

The following narrative relates to the history of my wife's accident and its myriad consequences, as I know them. Most of the detail was written down in diary form as it occurred. The rest of the tale is described more or less as it was eventually related to me by my wife, Margaret.

The dialogue is supplemented by narrative gleaned from all the people involved in caring for her subsequent to the accident. Supporting evidence is available for everything but my conjecture.

I am not medically qualified and have striven not to give an opinion that may be judged as a medical opinion. On the other hand, I am not too unintelligent about medical matters or anything else scientific, for that matter. If you read my recently published Sci-Fi book, '*Zondor the Great*' with it's novel theory on the time dimension, this will be sufficient to prove my point.

In the process of gleaning certain facts - together with what I fondly imagined were important details, I have, however sought medical and optometric advice. This was mainly in order to refute or substantiate certain medical arguments contained within the now infamous document that is loosely termed the 'Medical Report'.

The NHS administration comes under heavy fire for sucking all the money and professionalism out of the hospital service, but what do you expect from someone with my nearly forty years NHS experience. This covers from the good old days to the bad old days and I have seen it all happen.

The diary extract, that forms the history of the first four weeks or so post-accident happenings to my wife, is taken directly from my record of events. Everything else, apart from my personal comments on what I see as the devastating and mushrooming spread of NHS administration and its adverse effects on the care of our health, is supported by - often verbatim - extracts from my computer diary of subsequent events.

JG 2010

Chapter One
The Accident

It had rained heavily on the previous evening and everywhere in the city, the pavements were dappled with the usual puddles lying as traps for the unwary. Apart from that, the pedestrianised area of late 1990's Cardiff held many attractions and advantages for shoppers, including amongst them, the prestigious St David's Shopping Centre and eight or so historic Arcades of note.

It was the journey into town to get to them that was the main chore; partly because of the parking difficulties until the University students went home for Christmas. On that late November (25th), day at lunchtime, the town would be full of early Christmas shoppers. In any case, Thursday was 'Valleys Day' when the Welsh valley-people normally flooded into Cardiff in those days.

My wife and I have lived in Cardiff for over forty years now, so I guess that we know our way about the city. We have watched it grow and change from the coal and steel town of a bygone era to its present modern, business-oriented city with its attendant, though perhaps over-glamourised, Bay Area.

Earlier in the day, I had left the house at around nine-thirty to teach the largely un-teachable wrinklies how to use computers. The courses were held at one of the Community Education Centres on the Cardiff City outskirts. Most of the people who attended just wanted to be able to use a word-processing program to type a letter. Some had their own agenda.

I had been more or less forced into redundancy/early retirement from my secure professional job within the National Health Service some twelve years previously. This was, surprisingly, from what was perhaps regarded by my colleagues as 'a job for life'.

If this were not enough, I was one of the few people in the Cardiff hospital service at that time who held a 'higher' degree (MSc) in Management. But there you go!

Prior to the inauguration of the new-style post-1974 NHS, I had been seconded to a special team of lecturers. The primary aim of this team was to prepare key NHS personnel for the changes in the proposed new system of health care. But this dubious honour did nothing to save my particular post in the scheme of things to come.

In order to cope with the might of the medical profession, one of Julius Caesar's most powerful weapons of war was utilized by the new administration – 'Divide and Conquer'. Thus, 'Divisions of Medicine' were formed.

So, now, instead of targeting the administration for their new ventures, the medical fraternity fought against each other's specialty for a share of the diminutive 'cake'. This 'cake' was the amount of money available to fund new ideas, extra staff, new equipment and space.

Up until that time, there was always a little pot of money available for equipment and projects at the end of each financial year. Under the new administration, all hospital functions except administration were suddenly in deficit on their budgets at the end of each financial year.

At the time, everyone, including my professional colleagues, seemed a bit surprised when I took the offered early retirement without a fight. Yet, within a year, there were plenty of people in my medical scientific profession who would have loved the chance to follow my example.

In my totally biased view, their precarious predicament was created by the cost-cutting climate that had been generated within the NHS by the newly-introduced breed of administrators. It took several changes in Government (until 2010) for anyone in high office to comment on the destruction of our wonderful Health Service caused by such a policy.

The cuts in the NHS professions were needed in order to pay the huge administrative salary bill created by those 1974 changes to the structure of the NHS administration. The professional level at most risk under the new structure were those top-of-the-profession, mainly administrative posts, held by real, knowledgeable, fully qualified in their specialty and dedicated health-service professionals.

Administrators were invariably youngish people in smart suits. Their badge of recognition was a slightly lost, or vacant look as they wandered the corridors of the hospital clutching a sheaf of hurriedly assembled pieces of paper as they sought the venue for their next meeting. Nothing to do with patient care, of course.

One of these 'wonders' wandered into the Pathology Laboratory without any protective clothing. I asked him if he had been cleared by the Health and Safety people, then advised him to have a full set of 'jabs' if he did not wish to remain an unacceptable health risk to my staff.

He countered with a wish to see all the laboratory safety instructions pertaining to staff and working practices. He was totally unaware that a recent Health and Safety audit had commended that particular laboratory for achieving the requisite standard – one of the few in the UK at that time, as it happens.

He did not try that again. He got his own back as the administrator chosen to write my redundancy letter. Not only that, but for his trouble, he was paid a £3,000 bonus – roughly 25% of my annual take-home pay at the time.

So our glorious NHS became lumbered with 'Time and Motion' experts, 'Personnel Officers', 'Training Officers' and so on. These jobs alone made it impossible for the previously vital, health-oriented professional department managers (such as myself) - who helped make the NHS from scratch all those years ago in 1948 - to survive. And if you are asking the question, the answer is, 'Yes! I did join the NHS in 1948!

As far as NHS resources were concerned, those new administrative functionaries demanded space, secretaries and staff to do the work.

So they were an expensive addition to the health care scene and leant absolutely nothing to patient services directly.

Sadly, many of the specialist department heads affected by the new functionaries - such as myself, might have felt that their jobs must be safe when they were given special 'management' training by those same training officers. This was presumably in order to make them more efficient managers as well as making them more aware of where they fitted into the new system.

'And for my next trick? You are redundant!'

Part of the functions of those now technically redundant professionals had included providing specialty staff-training for the job, providing an emergency out-of-hours service, including holiday cover, controlling standards of work, staff promotion and health and safety considerations.

Also those key members of the hospital staff always sported the highest qualifications within their specialty. This latter was a vital ingredient for managing their service to an accountable high standard of excellence within their chosen field of expertise.

Suddenly, it was no longer possible for these whiz-gurus to hire and fire staff, arrange professional staff training, or even get a light bulb changed without it creating a mountain of paperwork. These functions had to be followed up with the usual time-wasting phone calls and budget committee meetings just to find out why nothing was happening to requisitions. It now took ten men seven days to change a light bulb! Really!

Worse was to follow. 'Planned Maintenance' was introduced. Apart from generating more administrative jobs, paper requisitions and high jinks, this meant that when things stopped working, it was even more difficult to get them fixed unless the failure coincided with the planned maintenance schedule. There were serious budget considerations for unplanned maintenance, if nothing else.

Administrators in NHS hospital authorities were paid a bonus for every job they were able to cut from the NHS budget. My laboratory professional and administrative post had become technically - though not practically - anachronistic some thirteen years prior to my going. I classed myself fortunate to have lasted so long. Several of my counterparts in the UK had already suffered my impending fate and moved on.

However, twenty plus years on, you will still find my mark on quite a few protocols that exist within the NHS despite the advent of computers and changes in medical practice. As I oscillate between GP Surgery and hospital clinic as an occasional patient now, I often see evidence of my personal innovations.

Few of the new breed of administrators will ever be able to make such claims. After all, they offer non-productive, non-patient services and thus they constitute the dead weight within the Health Service. It is a real tragedy that before the NHS had administrators, it was the pride of Europe – if not the World – as far as Health Services go.

Other changes in budget strategies gave some of my ex-colleagues early grey hairs and cause for concern about the provision of vital services.

Without my protection from 'the system', I heard that most of the department heads previously under my professional control retired on the grounds of ill-health within a few years of my going. They were sick of watching money that had been ring-fenced for a particular professional service being used to fund yet more administrative schemes instead.

My wonderful piece of equipment for screening for cancer cells was also redundant. It had been cobbled together from odd bits of spare laboratory equipment parts. My dissertation in support of my efforts would languish unnoticed in some Institute library. Technology would have moved on by the time it was rediscovered.

The electrophoresis tank I hand-made from a sheet of Perspex was moved to the new University Hospital when that became operative in the early seventies. There was nothing available commercially that could touch my tank for accuracy and reliability of its results, so I understand!

So, as you can deduce, it was the onward rush of the new ideology for administering health care with a pen and a book of rules that led inevitably to the redundancy of my prestigious post along with others in similar positions.

From that time onwards, the burgeoning spread of administrators, their plush offices, their secretaries and all the modern office equipment they desired, competed for scarce NHS resources along with the kidney dialysers, Prem. Baby incubators and operating theatre equipment plus the space needed to house them and their secretaries.

Sadly, my article on the subject in the British Medical Journal some six years prior to my redundancy, failed to impress sufficiently to change the order of priority - that today is still 'administrators first'.

Like the invasive bugs, MRSA and Clostridium dificile, these, to my mind parasitic elements, infested hospitals from 1974 onwards. They sucked the professionalism and the dedication out of the NHS and destroyed the whole ethos of our glorious health service in my perhaps too-biased opinion. But who cares about that?

Which is a pity, because there are still some high-quality dedicated professional people around. They are helping to push back the frontiers of medical science and medical practice even on their severely limited budgets.

Despite the cuts ordered by the government a few years ago, administrative costs went up to 14% of the total NHS spend. Yet, administrative costs prior to the 1974 changes had been only 3% of a much smaller spend. (This means that about £1.00 out of every seven spent on the care of your general health and welfare now goes on administrative costs! How ridiculous can you get?).

The Conservative Party Leader, David Cameron, in a statement given on TV in the run up to the 2010 General Election, pledged to do something about the heavyweight NHS bureaucracy. He does not have the remotest chance of success.

Even such dedication to a cause is bound to fail. The administrators are much too strong a group to be moved by any vote-seeking political party! Besides, the administrative group sponsors are, as you might have guessed, the administrative side of the Civil Service. So, if you have ever watched 'Yes, Minister' on TV, you will appreciate that, 'that is that', so to speak.

Look at it as slicing the head of one of those Gorgonic monsters from Greek mythology. As fast as you cut one head off, another three heads grow in their place.

Suppose you cut out the Chief Administrator post for a Health Authority. The three people below that post who are, say, responsible for finance, supplies and general administration will all need an extra allowance and more staff for doing their share of the top administrator responsibilities they inherit. So it ends up costing more.

The trick for guaranteed success is to take out alternative tiers below the Chief and thus reduce the size of the pyramid. In that way, you can save a lot of money, reduce the length of the paper-chasing information chain and obtain quicker responses as a result.

If you do away with all those committees and allow the paid hospital professionals a degree of discretion instead of a pair of handcuffs, you just might have a real health service that we can be proud of once again.

I was reminded of the 'control by committee' problem the other day when I read about some fraught lady trying to sue the NHS for the death of one of her loved ones. Apparently, a piece of equipment malfunctioned during the operation that the near relative was undergoing at the local hospital - with deadly results.

The NHS had already issued the usual advisory about the piece of equipment of course. In the old days, these notices were circulated quickly directly to the relevant department. I suspect that the vital piece of information never got further than some administrator's in-tray, destined for the next committee meeting. And so the doctors doing the operation would not know about the fault in the equipment they were using until the appropriate committee met before sending out the memo.

I used to serve on several of these new post-1974 Health Authority sub-committees. Well, fourteen, to be exact! No time to do any actual work, of course.

Amongst other things, we used to review all notifications about laboratory equipment faults. The meetings were held monthly, so the chore of processing information from top tier to bottom before sending the information to where it was actually needed took months rather than days.

At one meeting, a failure notice about a piece of equipment was on the agenda. Not one of the vast array of assembled professors and consultants or the administrative representatives realized that the equipment listed was **NOT** a piece of laboratory machinery. If that was the case, how on earth could a bunch of administrators at any level sort out where to send these vital notifications of problem areas?

Amongst other things, I was an equipment specialist and served on one of the British Standards' Committees for several years. So, inevitably, in the case of this failure notice, it was left to me - as the only one on the committee able to identify the right destination for the fault notice – to point out the error. The note about the fault referred to a piece of dental equipment. Not that my 'helpful' information endeared me to the committee - or the administrators - in any way. Rather the reverse!

In 1973, I was able to sign the order for the largest piece of laboratory equipment ever purchased in Wales at that time. By contrast, during my last year in my now redundant post (1987), I served on fourteen different committees but had no personal power to do anything job-related. I could not even purchase a new pencil except through an administrator. Funnily enough, I was not asked to sign a paper receipt for the pencil at that time.

So it is a tragedy for us all that too many of the breed are still in place today sucking the life-blood out of the NHS. And that happens before even one penny is spent on anything remotely medical, or on caring for your illness.

Together with their inevitable entourage of support staff, these ex-military and polished new university graduates blundered blindly into key professional areas after the big reorganisation took place in 1974. They are now firmly entrenched in the system like some alien race taking over the World. There is no antidote, save total eradication.

To be fair, some of the breed were very good at their job, but that hardly made up for the activities of the others. The words 'patients', 'health' and 'care' were as foreign to these latter as 'budget' and 'staff numbers' were the reality.

In 1987, in my retirement speech, as I stood next to the Health Authority General Manager and Chief Administrator (who was there to make the presentation), I orated:

'When I came into the Health Service in 1948, there were five hundred nurses for every administrator. Now, (1987) there are five hundred administrators for every nurse!'

This was greeted by loud cheers and jeers from the assembled colleagues and friends. They were all packed into the hospital Canteen to bid me farewell and to wish me well in my new venture. They knew the score!

I had spent most of the previous twenty-four years organizing the day-to-day laboratory service to many of the local Cardiff hospitals as well as running and taking part in the laboratory out-of-hours emergency service. If I had stayed for one more year, I might have received a medal for my forty-year's total service in the NHS.

In 1973, I published a 'Pay Review' article in one of the Health Service journals. In the article, I noted that the sudden rise in administrative staff pay from year 1972, reflected the Government's intention of passing the power base in the Health Service from the 'professionals', like doctors, nurses and department heads, to administrators.

This prophetic statement proved to be entirely correct. From a mere 3% of overall costs in 1973, administrative and clerical staff costs rose swiftly to a staggering 11% in the space of just a couple of years. Later it grew even higher to 14% of a much larger overall spend equivalent to nearly thirty percent pro-rata.

And the advent of the computer age tended to make things worse rather than better, since control through computer rather than a human interface, became somewhat easier.

Well, I should know because I used to review statistics for the Welsh Office returns every year. I have also lectured to Health Service managers on a variety of topics, including management issues.

You may wonder why I write on this subject so alien to the title of my book. Well, it is certainly not paranoia. By making me redundant, the NHS provided me with the best twelve years of my working life – my computer software business - until it was interrupted by Margaret's accident.

No, the diatribe was occasioned by the fact that similar cuts to my prestigious post occurred within other parallel professions. Those changes in allied NHS para-medical professions made a significant difference to the professional and technical services available within the NHS when my wife personally needed some of them.

So this change in NHS strategy appears to me to be quite pertinent to my story. However, these are my personal feelings and reflect on how I saw the system from my changed position and standing within the NHS at the time.

So, now you know.

But, enough of NHS history, though it establishes in some respects, my credo for future events. I was 'out' and had started to build up my one-man business - providing computer courses, network installations and computer advice in the South Wales area. It was wonderful.

My wife, Margaret, retired from her medical scientific post with the NHS in January 1998. This was after nearly thirty years of successful employment in various parts of the country. She was well liked and respected by her colleagues because of her organising ability and her charm.

More notably, due to her general speed around the workplace even at sixty plus years, she was known amongst the staff as 'the fastest thing on two legs'.

People could recognise the fast clip-clip of her shoes as she made her way around the corridors where she worked. She could get through a whole day's work by lunchtime and her part-time job was replaced with a full-timer when she left. So they say.

One special group of her old workmates would come over to the house for afternoon tea, or for an evening of gossip, (sorry, that should read 'conversation' or 'discussion' or 'exchange of ideas and information'). You probably know what ladies are like when they get together. I always kept well clear of the house on those occasions if possible.

After she retired from work, Margaret had developed a strategy for her weekly shopping trips into town, some five miles away. She would drive her VW Polo down North Road – the main A470 artery into Cardiff from the northern suburbs – and park in a side street close to a bus stop. Then she would catch the bus into town.

This procedure saved a longish walk from the house to and from our nearest bus stop with its twenty-minute service. It also gave her a choice of buses at much more frequent intervals than those in the outer suburbs.

Around noon on Thursday, 25th November 1999, Margaret was able to get off the No.27 Bus in Cardiff High Street, right beside 'Kitchens' shop. Here, she planned to buy a few Christmas stocking fillers for the culinary geniuses in our family who love kitchen gadgetry as much as cooking.

At the junction of High Street and St Mary's Street, (*see map on next page*), there is a left turn into Church Street - a fairly narrow, but pedestrianised short-cut lane to St John's Church. It also connects with Working Street that runs parallel to St Mary's Street. Two of Cardiff's main Department Stores fronted onto Working Street further down, though both did run through as far as St Mary's Street.

St Mary's Street was at that time however, a main thoroughfare through the city, running north to south from the High Street and Cardiff Castle. So, the bulk of shoppers tended to access the stores from the Working Street end where the pedestrianised environment made shopping so much more comfortable for browsing and window-shopping.

Church Street was a bustling alley at any time and no more so when there was an International Rugby match at the Millennium Stadium.

About halfway along - on the right hand side as you travel from the St Mary's Street end, is sited the famous (or infamous) 'Old Arcade' public house. On one memorable occasion, whilst supping a leisurely pint of local ale in that establishment, a French TV crew, who were in Cardiff for the Wales v France Six Nations rugby match, decided to film my friends and I as we chatted and drank. They were looking for local 'colour'!

I admit to having visited the Old Arcade on too few occasions - if only to sample Cardiff's local brew known as Brains SA. (Short for 'Skull Attack', I am assured and reliably informed, though I have never consumed enough of it on any one occasion to test the theory fully).

At that time, the 40cm square paviors that lined Church Street matched those throughout the pedestrianised area in town.

However, Church Street was always waterlogged after rain.

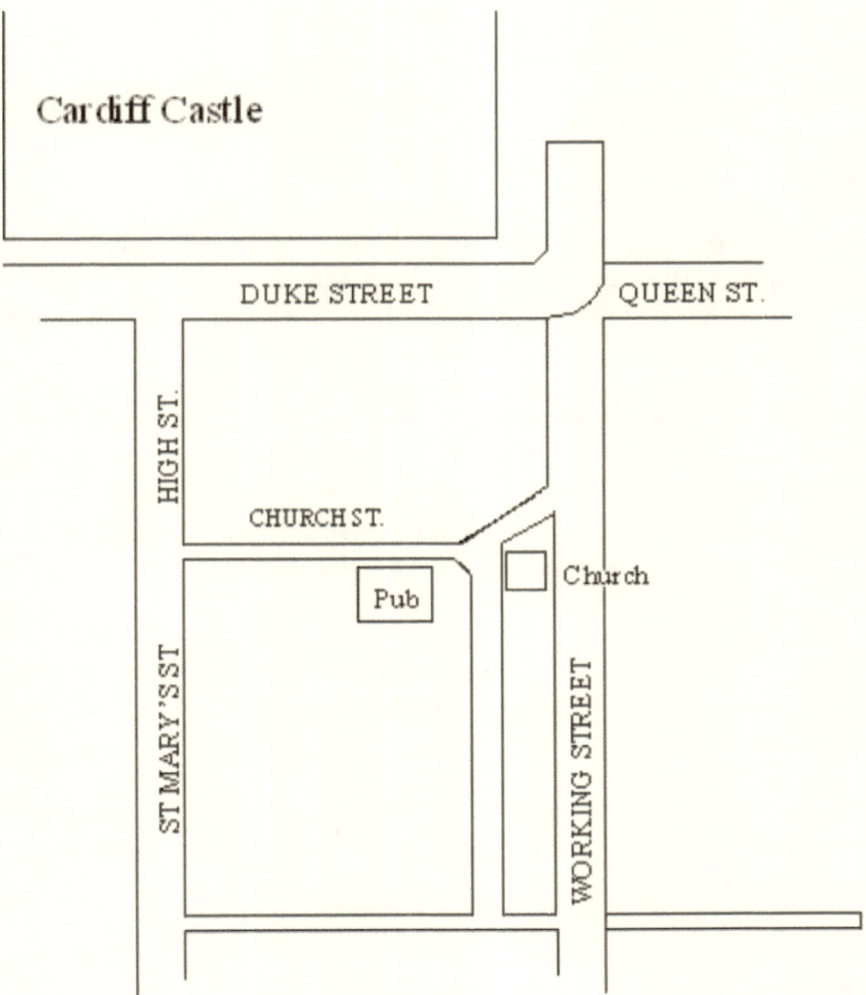

Successive upgrades to the properties on either side had helped loosen some of the blocks and spilled sand and cement into the drains. On rainy days, this allowed surface water to seep into the sand base under the blocks, making them unstable.

The center of the lane became a puddle-filled nightmare for pedestrians. Passage of heavy vehicles, such as the brewer's dray to the Pub had, over the years, subsequently squeezed some of the waterlogged base-layer sand onto the top of the blocks.

Since this was happening on a regular basis, it had the effect of further loosening the blocks in the process. Some blocks were even outlined in light silver-grey mud from the sub-soil that lay below the three inch sand layer.

Other parts of Cardiff's City Centre exhibited the same telltale signs of trouble for pedestrians. Fortunately, most of those pavings have since been replaced (between 2003 and 2009 - a mite too late for Margaret, unfortunately). Invariably, I would look for the 'silver lining' to detect the dangerous blocks.

From the Kitchen shop in St Mary Street, Margaret turned into Church Street on her way to Howells department store and Kayes shoe shop further down in The Hayes. She always kept well to the left in Church Street after rain. This was to avoid the three-foot-wide and six-foot long puddles in the centre of the lane in those days if it rained.

When my wife drew level with the bookshop, she crossed over to the other side of the street. We usually had a look in the window, or went inside to have a look at the book bargains in passing, but not today for Margaret. There was too much to do.

As she crossed over, she stepped onto a loose block and it tilted forward, raising its back edge some two to three inches, according to the marks on her trailing shoe.

Her trailing foot caught the back edge of the block and she was thrown forward in an arc, hitting her head as she fell, unable to break her fall because of her parcels and handbag.

She lay there for a few minutes to recover her senses and a passing couple helped her up. She felt dizzy and disorientated, so the helpful couple assisted her into the Café opposite the bookshop. They advised her to sit down and rest for a while before continuing her shopping.

The couple then helped brush off some of the wet sand, but there were also straight lines of a silver-greyish mud matching the outline pattern of the blocks. This mud would not brush off.

I was later able to ascertain that stepping onto the front edge of some of the blocks in Church Street raised the rear edge of the blocks by as much as two-and-a-half inches in the worst case. Since the trailing foot had already depressed the previous block-pavior, the difference in height between the two adjacent blocks could be anything up to a lethal five inches.

Several blocks in and around the area of Margaret's fall were loose and these could all be depressed at the front edge by two inches and raised at the back edge by at least two inches when stepped on in passage.

Crossing the street diagonally increased the risk of a trip because more than one block could tilt in either direction as it was stepped upon. Most of these blocks were outlined in the telltale silver-grey mud from below the sand base.

Thirty minutes later, after sipping a cup of black coffee, Margaret felt well enough to go out of the Café and to do some more shopping. The waitress who served her told me on a later visit to the Cafe that it was impossible to remember the incident because there were so many accidents in Church Street due to the state of the pavement in those days.

My wife told me that as she sat in the Café, she had watched the brewery dray deliver its load of beer barrels to the Old Arcade pub, before clattering back down Church Street.

The clatter was caused by the lorry as its wheels went over the paviors. They were lifting the back edge of each pavior and then depressing the front edge in succession – a bit like piano keys going up and down. She could see what happened to the paving blocks as other heavy lorries and vans moved over them.

The gift Margaret purchased in Howells Department Store was a sewing box. It was far too heavy and cumbersome for her to manage back to the bus stop so she arranged for it to be collected when I was next in town.

After she got to Kayes shoe shop, she felt a little unwell and was still feeling a bit shaken. Margaret decided to go home even though there were plenty of items on her list still to find. She caught the bus back to the street where the car was parked and drove home.

I came home from my teaching commitment at around quarter to four and sat down to watch 'Countdown' while Margaret made a cup of tea. This was our usual routine during the week. One significant action I had accomplished while I was out was to post the local Christmas cards that had 'Scout Stamps' on them, though the consequences did not become apparent for some time.

The local Scout Association charge about half the cost of a second class stamp to deliver local Christmas cards every year. Cards have to be available for sorting some time between late November and early December and we had completed most of these cards the night before so that they would be ready to post in the special boxes in the morning.

Margaret told me about her accident and how the couple had helped her into the Café and then showed me her stained overcoat and her scuffed shoes – all more or less ruined. I suggested that we try to have the coat cleaned but reckoned that the squared pattern of the light grey mud-stains would take a bit of shifting, though the remaining sand should drop off with brushing.

There was not much that could be done with the shoes. The top of one shoe was badly scored in a diagonal line right across the top face and the toe, some two to three inches from the tip. The toe of the other low-heel shoe had been completely demolished as if it had been compressed, concertina fashion.

After that incident, every time I went into town, I would check to see what progress had been made on repaving or repairing the street, but for the next two years, there was little or none. However, Church Street has since been the subject of a brand new pavement upgrade with the surface now laid in granite 'sets'.

Note. I have taken photographs in Church Street on regular occasions since the accident - the first in early December and the second in

early January 2000 and the third towards the end of the month. After that it was about once a fortnight. There had been no maintenance to the area visible in that time period. If anything, the state of the paved area had deteriorated further.

Those photographs were submitted as evidence eventually in support of Margaret's Case against Cardiff City Council.

Back home, little knowing that Margaret's life as we knew it would be irrevocably changed forever within a mere six hours, we prepared and ate our evening meal. Afterwards I cleared the dishes into the dishwasher except for the pans. Margaret always washed those in the sink bowl.

She reminded me that it was Thursday and she would be going straight out to the 7pm Church Meeting at our Church on Whitchurch Common – just over two miles away.

Margaret always took a keen interest and often an active part in those meetings. She was a House Group leader for the Church and had also just been elected to the post of Leprosy Mission Treasurer.

Several years previously, Margaret had been appointed as Treasurer for National Children's Homes in the Cardiff area, but gave that up when NCH changed their system. She was very good at figures and lists and protocols for her NHS professional job and used these same skills at home for sorting out and checking the Barclaycard, the Bank Statement and shopping bills for filing at home.

At the time of the accident Margaret was Chairman Elect for our local Floral Decoration Society, a member of two gardening clubs and a member of the local National Trust group. She also attended a Keep-Fit club, went swimming and occasionally, line-dancing.

These activities were just a few of her interests however and in many ways, she was 'the best thing since sliced bread' to her wide circle of friends.

Margaret was generous with her time to people who needed her support. I could never really believe the work she was able to get through in a day, or a week - and she enjoyed it all into the bargain.

My role in her busy life was to supply the logistics. I made things for her various activities, or worked out travel arrangements, typed letters and did some DTP on my computer.

We have a largish garden where we shared activities. I mowed the lawns and took care of any tree pruning and grew the vegetables and fruit.

Margaret tended the flowers in all the borders, the pots, the hanging baskets, the house floral decorations and the greenhouse. Though I somehow managed to grow greenhouse tomatoes and cucumbers in late Spring and Summer after she had cleared all the tender plants to their outside habitats.

The house and garden were full of flowers in season and the whole place was like a small public park in some respects.

Each year, we forayed out into the World for three or four weeks, exploring places of historical, or cultural interest.

We have explored the waterways of many countries in Europe and in China, Russia and its satellites - not forgetting the UK. There were regular weekend visits to friends and family and also weekend breaks in the Spring and Summer and seasonal breaks just after Christmas and at half terms.

We also visited National Trust properties and County Shows. As it is supposed to be for many semi-retired people, life had become one long holiday in some ways. Margaret had done most of the choosing and organising of these activities.

Added to it all were her music interests (Leeds International Piano Competition and Cardiff Singer of the World) and her floral interests (Area and National events with NAFAS). Then there was the entertaining of friends and family and all the associated phone calls.

While Margaret was busy with her life, I played with my computer (well, I ran my small computer software business), did some teaching and computer installations and watched a bit of rugby now and again. A dull, sober life by comparison.

If you gain the impression that we lived busy lives prior to the accident, then let me remind you that, until a few months before the accident, Margaret worked part-time as well as coping with all her activities. Meanwhile I merely ran my computer software training business. But all that was to change in a flash, as you will see.

Chapter Two
Margaret Disaster

I had served in the Royal Army Medical Corps for my two years of National Service in the early fifties of the twentieth century. I followed this by serving another fourteen years in the RAMC Territorial Army. One of the things I had forgotten from that training in the intervening forty or fifty years was to give head-injury patients very close observation for the first twenty-four hours in case there was an internal bleed.

Well, it was a long time ago!

This omission became obvious to me later when Margaret was late getting home from her Church Meeting. I started to worry a little. She was not usually this late coming home from that Church Meeting or any other evening activity, come to think of it.

Margaret arrived home at some time after ten o'clock instead of around nine.

She started to explain to me that one of her elderly church friends - a widow - desired a lift home from someone to take her to her out-of-town abode, since it was such a stormy night. The alternative for the lady was to take a bus into town, stand around waiting in the wind and rain and then take another bus out of town in the other direction – not good options for someone of her years.

Although the lady's destination was four or five miles in the opposite direction to the mere two miles we live away from the Church, Margaret offered to take this friend home. Which is fairly typical of Margaret's caring stance in the World.

Whenever I think of that journey in such awful weather, I shudder. The journey from Whitchurch Common to the Drope Farm area on the outskirts of Cardiff was along narrow, often poorly lit roads. The road went down a windy hill, over a level crossing and then over the River Ely humped bridge. It then climbed up a steep, equally windy hill on the other side, where it was always dark due to overhanging trees.

What with the high wind and the heavy rain, there was the ever-present danger of scraping the car wings on the concrete block wall that lined one side of this narrow country road.

During the day, it would not be too difficult, but at night and in the middle of a storm, it must have been hell.

After dropping the lady off at her home, Margaret wisely decided to return via the longer motorway route using the Ely Link Road to the M4.

Some time after her recovery from the accident and when some of her memory returned, she told me that because of the weather, she prayed all the way home since she did not feel too great. It had been a long, tiring and eventful day.

I opened our big front door and switched on the outside light when I heard the car draw up. Then I went indoors to put the kettle on to make a cup of tea. Meanwhile, Margaret parked her car in its normal place on the slope in front of the garage on our forecourt.

She came in all of a rush and started to tell me why she was so late getting home. I asked her which way she had gone and Margaret looked at me as if I had not really understood what she had been saying.

Suddenly, she stopped and stared balefully at me. I was quite taken aback. She looked obviously tired and seemed unable to continue the conversation. It was as if she had 'lost the plot'.

'*Oh, you are stupid*', she said. '*You are talking rubbish!*', and went off upstairs in high dudgeon with her cup of tea in her hand, to get ready for bed.

I was so surprised and a bit upset at her reaction. But it was so unlike her. She is normally such a loving person and we have always got on so well during the previous forty-three years of our marriage. I wondered if something had upset her and never even thought about the accident.

Margaret feels happier and sleeps sounder if she has a regular change of sleeping direction while I just need a bed – any bed. She had decided to sleep in the middle bedroom with its north-south aspect and I said my goodnight and went downstairs to watch the end of the film on TV. It was a little after eleven and the film finished at about twenty past.

As I came up, I heard a strange noise and Margaret called me to say she felt sick. I hastily went downstairs again to get the basin and some towels and got to her just in time. She was violently and uncontrollably sick and continued in this vein for quite a few minutes.

My brain clicked into gear as it started to put all the circumstances of her day together. As soon as there was some respite from the constant heaving, I phoned the night GP service and explained about her accident less than twelve hours ago.

The doctor arrived in about ten minutes and immediately called for an ambulance. Margaret quite lucidly explained to this doctor about her accident and gave some of her scanty medical history (she was hardly ever ill) when he enquired.

I started to gather some warm clothes for Margaret and some toiletries and put them in a plastic bag as I realized the consequences. By the time the ambulance arrived she was ready to go. I followed afterwards in my car as she was taken to the A & E Department of the University Hospital about three miles away.

In the ambulance, Margaret gave the paramedics much the same information she had imparted to the GP. She did the same when the Receiving Doctor in the Accident Unit asked her more or less the same questions.

Margaret was subsequently admitted to the University of Wales Hospital (Ward C7, assigned to a Consultant Physician – Dr Geraint Olds). She had previously been in excellent health and was not under **any** treatment for **any** medical condition at that time, unless you consider natural tears for her dry eyes as medication. So this was quite a traumatic experience for us both.

In the Accident Unit, I hung around Margaret's trolley, giving her reassurance whenever I could that she was in safe hands.

She fell asleep, so I rushed back home, arriving at just before 4am. My first computer class was at ten so I put the alarm on for 7am and went straight to sleep.

During my army service all those years ago, I had quickly realised the value of being able to sleep at any hour of the day or night and had taught myself to wake at a given time.

With a bit of practice, I was able to sleep for as little as five minutes if necessary. It took no time to learn how to wake up for night guard duty ten minutes before I was due on post. This facility came in handy a few years later when our two boys were born.

During my employment in the NHS, the ability to sleep at will had also come in useful. I was part of an emergency call team for seventeen years and on one occasion had worked throughout the weekend without a break even for meals. Those days have long since gone thankfully in the NHS and changes in working practices now prohibit those long stretches of duty.

Although my army service was more than fifty years ago, I can still wake up just a few seconds before the alarm goes when I have need of a wake-up call - such as when we have a plane to catch to go on holiday. On that Friday morning, I woke just before the alarm clock beeped its 7am warning.

Breakfast for me was straightforward. Cornflakes mixed with a little muesli, covered in milk.

This repast was followed by a few spoonfuls of yoghurt and a mug of half-and-half milky coffee. The coffee was made with original powdered

Nescafe and a teaspoonful of sugar and then cooked in the Microwave for exactly two minutes. (Well, what do you expect with my scientific background? At least I stopped short at weighing out the cornflake portions).

In those pre-accident days, I had no need for all the pills I now take some ten years later. Such is the plight of the carer and the onset of old age.

The house felt empty and without Margaret, the whole place sounded hollow. Most of my actions were automatic and I picked up my bag with all the gear for my computer courses after checking with the hospital by phone.

Margaret had been admitted to one of the Wards and was on a drip. She was due for a brain scan later in the day. They reckoned that she had suffered a brain haemorrhage that they referred to as a 'stroke' but were unable to say more than that at the time.

I knew all about strokes from some of my Grass Bowls friends when they paid unscheduled visits to the hospital where I worked for many years. After enquiring if there was anything Margaret needed, I said I would call in on the way back from my class at lunchtime.

Twelve o'clock couldn't come soon enough for me and I was signed out and up to the hospital by quarter past midday. I knew my way around the hospital and soon found the Ward.

Not knowing what to expect, I gingerly entered the small Ward at the far end of the corridor housing the nursing station and ancillary rooms. Margaret was sitting up in pole position on the left as I entered the Ward, with just a window on the other side of her.

This gave her quite a spacious area round her bed and a nice outlook if she cared to glance that way. I have no sense of smell due to chronic nasal polyps and so did not appreciate the rare atmosphere of the place, but our friends appraised me of it after their visits.

It was, apparently quite an odorous Ward, but with patients having no control over their functions, I guess that even when catheterised, it was probably difficult for the few Ward staff to cope with all the body needs.

Margaret did not recognise me and her speech was seriously affected. Once she started speaking, however, she babbled on repeating herself a few times and going over the same things again and again. All simple short words like a very young child.

She looked a bit disorientated but was quite settled. There was a dull, glazed look to her eyes and her inner 'light' appeared to have gone out. Margaret's main topics were that 'HE' had been in and 'SHE' was doing something.

I later pieced it all together. 'HE' was male – probably one of the doctors and 'SHE' was the nurse. Then there were others such as 'HER' who was a female visitor and 'HIM' who was myself, or any other male visitor.

Basically, those were Margaret's 'vocabulary' at the time – made up from words that she had heard other people say when they were attending her. For all intents and purposes, her brain had been wiped clean.

I was devastated.

The diagnosis was given as 'post-traumatic brain injury'.

My doctor friend, Chas later explained to me that after a brain injury, any spilled blood produces a chemical that sort of 'eats' the brain cells that come into contact with it. Meanwhile, the leak of blood may spread slowly into the rest of the brain, knocking out vital functions as it goes, until the blood eventually clots and stops its spread.

He went on to say that many elderly people are prescribed drugs that stop the blood from clotting – usually for heart complaints. This might also be a post-operative measure to deal with clots in the blood, or could be given as part of a regime to thin the blood and reduce the blood pressure of people of my age who may have persistent high blood pressure.

There have been some high-profile cases of prominent figures in our society who have hit their heads accidentally. They subsequently died because the blood in their brain failed to clot quickly and efficiently due to medication they were taking such as warfarin.

I told Chas, that Margaret was not on any drugs.

As far as I was aware, Margaret had never had high blood pressure (that the doctors referred to as 'hypertension') and had never been treated with drugs to prevent her blood from clotting. I expect that was why she was still alive.

She had previously been in excellent health throughout her working life. Now, as she was, surrounded by the inevitable plastic tubing and wires that cris-crossed her body, she was drip-fed for about two days and fitted with a catheter.

Her blood pressure, pulse and respiration were monitored and the levels recorded manually on a regular basis. She was given tablets to control her blood pressure and also for water retention.

When I arrived on the Ward, I could hear the young lady in the cubicle opposite the entrance thrashing about on her bed. The curtains parted to allow the nurses in to look after her. The youngish lady was bare from the waist downwards with her night attire up round her middle.

The tabloid newspaper on the end of her bed caught my eye as a bare foot kicked it in passing. As the folded paper slipped gracefully to the floor, it opened up to the front page.

In emblazoned headlines two or three inches high, it carried the two words:

'MARGARET DISASTER'

The words were placed one under the other with a recent photo of Princess Margaret set beside them. But I just saw the words. Nothing else.

They hit me like a bullet. I just stood and stared at them as the cubicle curtains were drawn across my vision.

There were a few things to remember to bring in for Margaret on my next visit and I hastily made a list. I added deodorant air-wick to that list.

Just then, a well-dressed, portly, elderly, almost bald man breezed into the Ward and made his way down to the far end of the room. He looked a bit like the guy who controls Morse in the detective series of that name on TV. The lady in the bed he visited looked well cared for and of much the same build. I thought they looked a perfect matching couple.

The man embraced the patient and from the nature of the embrace, I assumed that she was his wife. It is difficult to describe their attitude to each other. The only way I can really describe it is like a Golden Labrador greeting its long-lost master or mistress. I feel sure that if the man had a tail, he would have wagged it off in the first minute.

The couple were both animated to extremes and obviously more than fond of each other. I could not imagine Margaret and I acting like that in public.

Every so often, someone would check the drip-feed to Margaret's arm. At the same time, the nurse would note her blood pressure (which was very high). I could find no fault with the medical and technical nursing she was receiving.

Maybe at this stage I should have declared an interest to the Ward staff as ex-NHS of nearly forty years standing. For I have been exposed to many aspects of the health care scene within the hospital environment from time to time as an unwitting observer.

Another nurse came in to the Ward just then and came over to Margaret. That nurse took her blood pressure and I could see that it was still quite high. I could also observe that the charts behind the bed-head showed that blood pressure, pulse and respiration were being monitored on a very regular basis.

Margaret was on a drip and receiving some medication via that route, but was not allowed food. Inability to swallow is apparently a common result of a stroke or head injury. The doctors were taking no chances of her choking to death if she could not swallow her food.

I left the hospital just before Margaret was taken down for her brain scan and did a bit of weekend food shopping before coming home to our empty house. Then I took hold of the phone, sat down on the bottom of the stairs and began to make a few phone calls to our family and to close friends.

We have a lot of friends whose numbers are stored on the handset and this makes it easy to communicate with them. I soon exhausted that list and got out our address book to contact some more.

Then I had a brainwave of sorts. If I finished writing the Christmas cards and sent them out early, I could use my computer to make a short letter on card to enclose with the Christmas cards. Then those people who lived outside Cardiff would all get to know at the same time with minimal effort on my part and I could devote more time to my dilemma.

Not long afterwards, I realised that I had not eaten for some time. I prized some homemade soup out of the freezer, cooked myself an omelette and some potatoes and did some custard to go with a chopped banana. A meal at least! This almost exhausted my complete range of culinary skills.

Unlike my two sons, I have never developed any skills in that direction. My mother was a good food provider and Margaret was up to cordon-bleu standards at times. So I never had the need.

My mother could only make lumpy custard and so while I lived at home, I developed a scientific technique for making smooth custard, hence the skill.

I am allergic to meat and meat products so I would make myself an omelette if there were no suitable fish alternative. Hence that particular skill.

However, I have burned water before on occasion, so my culinary talents do not extend much beyond those two pale yellow items.

Perhaps it has something to do with the colour.

Despite not getting to bed until nearly one thirty in the morning, I was in the hospital just after eight on Saturday morning with the extra clothes Margaret needed and some stick deodorant and air-wick.

Sister was on duty at the nurse's station and I wished her, 'Good morning' as I passed by. No one asked me who I was, or why I was there. The same nurse that I had seen taking blood pressure etc on the previous day was at Margaret's bed doing the same routine.

Just then, a fly sprang into life.

The nurse smiled and said to me, 'Oh, look. There's a fly'.

To which I replied, 'Oh, yes. He's just been having his breakfast off your dirty bloodstained drip stand'.

End of conversation – forever!

That nurse never ever spoke to me again on any of my frequent visits for the rest of the time Margaret was on that Ward.

Later in the week I felt vindicated. The drip-stand was being taken from the sluice-room all sparkling and clean. At the same time, one of the nurses was spraying the stand with bacterial inhibitor.

With me on that visit, I had brought one of our small brown cases carefully packed. In it, there were several changes of basic underwear, a couple of nighties and toiletry items including a toilet bag to hold all the small stuff. It included a list of items and I added to that list the things in the locker that I had taken in on my trip to the Accident and Emergency Unit.

I also brought Margaret's eye-drops - natural tears prescribed by the University Hospital Eye Department earlier in the year in order to counteract dry eyes.

The staff-nurse took charge of the eye-drops. That particular hospital's Eye Department had prescribed the drops previously. Yet those drops would still need vetting by that same hospital Pharmacy Department to ensure that they did not interfere with other drugs prescribed for Margaret's current ongoing treatment.

The Registrar bumped into me (not literally) as I was on my way out. My arms were laden with things to wash and a list of items for the next day, but I introduced myself as Margaret's husband.

He gave me a little bit of information about Margaret's general condition but no details about the scan or prognosis or treatment. After all, I was just a bystander about to become a Carer. He had seen it all before.

Back home, I had started on the phone-calls again between the visits, checking Margaret's diary in order to cancel all her commitments. I understand that some people actually cried when they heard the news and others found that they could not continue their work when I told them about the accident.

There's love for you!

After making myself some lunch, I went back into the hospital.

My sister arrived from up-country in the late afternoon and I settled her in before getting fish and chips from our local Chippie as usual for Saturday night's supper. Since she was aware of the tradition, it all went off alright.

I had already warned her that she would be sleeping in the bed in the twin-grandchildren's nursery room and to get a good night's sleep before they arrived next day. We visited the hospital and my sister was pleasantly surprised at how bright Margaret was on that second evening in hospital.

Later in the evening, the Registrar was able to tell me that the brain scan showed that there was a small clot deeply seated within the frontal lobe of the brain, so I gathered that it was in line with the area of Margaret's skull that hit the pavement in Church Street.

I am suggesting that as a possible fact because no one ever actually inferred that it was and it was not taken into account in any further examinations by anyone – a point that irked me somewhat as will become apparent as my tale unfolds.

Margaret's blood pressure was still running high in the evening, but she looked more herself, though there was no sign of any memory returning. Although she was a bit shaky on her legs, there was no paralysis or other physical disability such as those normally associated with a stroke.

There was however a definite speech problem and severe loss of memory that I thought might be 'amnesia' due to the severe blow to the head. But then, what do I know about anything? The loss of memory included most words and as we discovered a few days afterwards, all the numbers and also all the letters of the alphabet.

Considering her role in society as an instructor, speaker, treasurer, worldwide traveler, classical music lover and avid reader of books, this was a terrible blow to what was for us all, a busy, interesting - even exciting life. The immediate loss to myself, not to mention the community was to say the least, disastrous.

Three visits a day was about as much as I could manage.

I finished the Christmas cards and inserted my little note about the accident and posted them all on the following Monday morning. With hindsight, I might have guessed what would happen. A couple of days later, as the post arrived at its destination, the phone calls started.

On Sunday morning, I checked about the eye-drops because Margaret pointed to her eyes when I arrived. I was told that Pharmacy had not yet approved them for use and, since it was Sunday it was now too late to get approval. Well, I can tell you how I reacted, but you don't really want to know.

Margaret was ashamed of me and for me, poor lamb. I would have liked to bite out my tongue at that moment in time, even though I was in the right to complain. Not that I ever use four-letter words. Mine are longer and all in the OED (and I think they are more effective for that reason).

Back home, the family arrived from Reading and I realized that I would have to give my son, Pete instructions about getting to the hospital. He still knew his way about the area from living in Cardiff as a youth and I foresaw no problems.

I was also able to give my son details of where to park and how to get quickly to the Ward in Cardiff's most prestigious University Hospital of Wales. He had lived in Cardiff for most of his youth years, but things had changed in the fifteen years he had been away from the city.

I looked after the twins while he and his wife, Jennifer, visited.

I expect that it was a tearful reunion because both my son and daughter-in-law love Margaret dearly. It would be a bit of a shock to see their lively reliable and loving Mum and Mum-in-law laid so low.

Apparently, Margaret seemed pleased to see her eldest son and I wondered if there had been a spark of recognition when they met.

People talk to their loved ones as if there is nothing wrong with the communicative side after they have overcome the first hurdle. So there was really no way of knowing how they were perceived when someone they knew so well had lost their memory. I hoped that all the visits from dear friends and close family would do something to jog Margaret's memory. Otherwise it would be a long time before we saw any improvement.

My grandson, Terry, who was only two and a half at the time, summed it all up in one clear and precise sentence.

'*Gran'ma in 'opital. No'ch vewy wewll*'.

I nearly cried.

The family came equipped with food, but I had already put salmon on the menu for dinner and the house was in order to cope with their visit. This was no mean thing to organise or achieve under the circumstance. All the toys have to be instantly available for the twins as they rush through the front door. The beds and cots were all ready and made up to ensure peace and harmony throughout their stay.

Further to this, I was now getting lots of phone calls. Whilst cleaning and cutting the salmon into fillets I received no less than ten phone-calls. It took me two hours to do a twenty-minute job.

My daughter-in-law showed me how to use our washing machine so that I would be able to take care of all the laundry that was building up in the clothes' basket. I filled in some of the background to what had happened and outlined the present situation.

I was used to dealing with the semantics and logistics of the family visits. The additional responsibility for the food was not a problem since both my son and daughter-in-law were self-taught gourmet cooks. My sister was no mean slouch in the kitchen either.

It was on that Sunday - the third day after admission - that Margaret was tried out on solid foods.

Unlike the stroke people, she had still apparently, retained the ability to swallow. Classical stroke victims usually lose this ability and are drip-fed until that ability returns. But Margaret's stroke was due to the fall and subsequent trauma when she hit her head and not induced by any clinical manifestation.

The addition of two cook experts made a huge difference to my diet that weekend and my body was able to stock up a bit while the family were there. I still found myself getting to bed late and rising early to try to fit in a few more chores. I needed to keep the house presentable for visitors and to catch up with the dishes and clothes washing.

On Monday morning when I visited Margaret, I discovered that the eye-drop problem had actually been resolved on Friday shortly after the drops had reached Pharmacy. Typically, the person given the information failed to pass it on. This really got me going and I realised that something had to be done.

The Ward was run efficiently enough for most things but was lacking in the bits that make life bearable for the patient. It just needed a bit more tlc and attention to the minutia. I put a bit more pressure on the medical as well as the nursing staff to perform over that eye-drops incident and mentioned a few other things into the bargain.

On one of my visits, (it must have been Tuesday when Margaret felt a bit better) I was amazed to see that Mr. Churchman, the Minister from our Church had arrived.

Margaret was absolutely delighted and although she could not express that delight her pleasure was obvious to everyone.

That he had taken time out of his busy schedule to visit her was a measure of his feelings for one of his flock. I was aware that he did more than his share of visiting the sick and the needy.

Margaret's friend Carrie, of forty-odd years acquaintance, arrived from Warwickshire after lunch on Tuesday and she moved into the bed just vacated by my sister. With my son's family on the way home, she was assured of unbroken sleep.

That lady came with frozen food - home-cooked of course and I put most of it in the freezer. Carrie had brought a fish pie for our evening meal and so no fish and chips for tea.

The lady was a staunch friend. She and I empathised in a non-sexual way, even though she was very cuddly.

On the hospital front, things were looking up.

This 'new era' could have been attributed to standard practice but perhaps I should tell you that two doctor friends of ours - one a top consultant with a world-wide reputation and the other a GP – had visited Margaret on the Sunday morning.

I was not there as it happened, because I went to Church after my early morning visit as we usual do on Sundays. At the church, I thoughtfully asked the Minister for permission to put a small notice in the reception area of the Church at the front door.

My return home was delayed by many of Margaret's friends who wanted to know what had happened and where she was. I hoped that my little notice would reduce the number of people asking how Margaret was doing.

It turned out to be just as well that I was not at the hospital while my medical friends, Chas, Laura his wife and their GP daughter, Helen were there.

Well, you know what doctors are like. I suspect that my two medical friends examined all the charts and patient data as they assessed Margaret's situation. These big Consultants have that 'quality' air about them too, that is always impressive if not intimidating.

Their presence must have created quite a stir amongst some of the nursing and medical staff in the hospital as word of the visit got out.

Some of the other patients thought it was a specialist team about to operate. There were several other groups of visitors throughout the day of course, including my son and his family, as I mentioned earlier.

On my Monday evening visit, the Registrar had quizzed me about my two medical friends. Naturally, I played down their visit, saying that they were just some friends of ours. It is easy to become embroiled in politics in these situations if you handle it insensitively. He seemed satisfied and pleased that I was not trying for second opinions through the back door.

The Registrar was getting used to my frequent visits and so, when I met him on Tuesday morning, I asked for a meeting with the consultant - Dr Olds to discuss prognosis amongst other things. My efforts to arrange it through Sister on Friday and Saturday had failed miserably, leading to my wasting time - time I could hardly afford with my increasingly busy schedule - waiting for him to appear on two occasions already.

The meeting was duly set for noon on Wednesday, which was the following day.

Wednesday dawned slowly. I could hardly wait.

Carrie said that she would leave for home that morning. When she made tracks for home, there was only myself again to inhabit the house. After having a full-house, so to speak, the house felt more empty than before. I was all set to go to the hospital for the twelve o'clock meeting.

Midday could not come quickly enough. I had one quick customer call to make on the way to the hospital and I still managed to arrive well before twelve.

The drip-set and drip-stand had vanished. All the plastic tubes had gone and Margaret was back on solid food. The 'No Food by Mouth' sign had been taken down as well. 'Get Well' cards and flowers had started to appear on the windowsill as well as around the bed head.

Sister showed me into one of the meeting/waiting rooms and Dr Olds duly arrived. He mentioned about my two doctor friends and I parried that with, 'Oh, them. They were only here to visit my wife. I gave them strict instructions about conduct because she is **your** patient'.

Needless to say, he relaxed.

I was able to give him some of the background details of what had happened to my wife. At the same time, I let drop that his big boss was someone I used to know quite well in the old days and perhaps the boss would like to know that my wife was in hospital on his next visit to the ward. I was aware, however that my old medical acquaintance was away on holiday for two weeks.

Feeling slightly guilty at such blatantly arrogant behaviour, I was afraid that my face would colour. I am usually quite a gentle guy - not used to doing such dastardly deeds. Without Margaret to add her little control words, it all came out. Just shows what we humans are capable of doing for our loved ones when placed in such a dire situation.

Dr Olds was quite surprised with my little bit of accurate medical knowledge of the injury site and he responded with details of what the scan had revealed, confirming what my doctor friend, Chas had suggested might be the case.

My remark that I had been puzzled because of the treatment regime - or lack of it - and that those details explained his handling of the case to me also surprised and pleased him. But after all, I had been well primed by my friend Chas before the meeting.

Dr Olds said that he thought that his Registrar had apprised me of the situation. I smiled in that way people do in organ-grinder and monkey situations.

You may think badly of me if you like. Let me tell you that I was paranoid about the situation and was singularly engaged in getting the best possible care for my wife. I was also tired out after a weekend of twins, family, phone calls and visitors.

It was an opportunity to drop names of other important medical friends and to air my petty grievances about the state of the ward (very quietly of course). Well, even though I was ready to charge in with all cylinders firing, I took it very gently - just enough to make the point in a simple inoffensive way.

Afterwards, I was to realise just how important this meeting had been. It must have inspired a high degree of confidence in my integrity at least.

Knowing that my wife was lactose-intolerant and allergic to cows milk and all cows-milk products, I brought in some goats yoghurt next day for her to use on her cornflakes at breakfast. Fortunately, the cows-milk allergy does not extend to goat's dairy products. It has something to do with the size of the molecules of the species-specific lactose sugar.

I was aware of this feature of lactose during my NHS Laboratory life. One of my staff did his research on the different types of lactose enzymes that are present in living entities. Since then, other studies on the subject have highlighted the chemical differences.

Margaret had complained of feeling 'ungry' apparently, ('ungry' is a local Cardiff word in the language of the Cardies) and now she cried as she told me about it. She could not understand about the drip feed or why she had been without food for so long.

Her tears dried when she said that she felt alright now that she had been fed on proper food at last.

Her mood swings were tremendous and it was difficult to hold on to reality while she swayed from over-zealous excitement to bitter tears and recriminations.

Probably due to my attitude at the interview with the consultant, things happened. My comments on the occasional errors and my critical stance on Ward hygiene causing pressure to have things improved must have jarred a few nerves. There were some positive results. People either got used to the smell of the ward, or it diminished.

I plumped for the latter reason because, to my pleasure and amazement, the whole ward had been cleaned up and the beds supplied with brand-new linen and bed-covers.

Even the screen curtains had been changed.

The room looked brighter.

This could have been a normal happening, I realized but it was a happy coincidence after my hints and asides.

To my astonishment, Sister said, 'Good morning Mr Greenridge,' when I breezed in - and produced a pleasant smile to go with the greeting.

On the treatment front, the medics and therapists had confirmed that Margaret had retained her ability to swallow. This was despite the occasional telltale secretion of spittle from the right side of her mouth (something fairly common in stroke patients, I understand). So things were improving slowly.

Margaret had learned a few more words and told me again that she was 'ungry'. The word still had that certain Cardiff flavour about the accent. I supposed that this was probably taken from the ladies who brought the first food. But then, perhaps it was the consultation with the dietician concerning things she could eat because of the news of her allergy to cows milk and cows dairy products.

On the up side, our home economics friend Ellen Rowe arrived at our house with a blackberry and apple pie. This I rather greedily divided up into six pieces when it might have done eight at a pinch. I did not see the point of having it eight times when six would see it all off. When it was finished, it would have done its job admirably.

The pieces, except for the one I would have for dinner, filled the empty but washed-out 1 Kg. margarine box and went in the freezer. Spaced nicely between other things, I would have a splendid selection of 'afters'. Thus, my scratch evening meal should never get boring.

I also picked up a pizza base from Safeway. Whatever happened to the tuna pizzas I have had before? They do plenty of other toppings, but no tuna! All that mercury in the tuna flesh, I suspect.

How I wish they were so strict about potato crisps with sprayed-on fancy-named flavours full of E-numbers! No wonder some young children feel aggressive with all those chemicals inside them!

Offers kept coming in all week for help of any kind.

People asked about visiting Margaret.

Unlike some people I have known, the only restriction I put on visiting was number of people and length of stay (no more than two at a time for no more than ten minutes). This ensured that Margaret never felt too tired after visits and got a lift from seeing new faces.

I was visiting mainly outside normal visiting-hours myself. No one seemed to mind. This assumed freedom allowed me to fit in visits between contract-work. Consequently, Margaret's numerous friends could go in normal visiting-hours without clashing with my visits.

A chap I used to bowl with in the Glamorgan Pairs Competition suffered a stroke several eons ago. His wife forbade anyone from the Bowls Club to visit. I was a bit upset about it in view of my NHS background but there was nothing I could do without upsetting his family.

Fortunately, he made a good recovery but like many males who suffer a stroke, he was left with a short fuse on his temper.

Mostly, this phenomenon is caused by the frustration of trying to convey even the simplest message or salutation.

My bowls partner could say a person's surname, but had to spell out their first name by drawing it on his palm with his finger. With all the Jones's and Williams's and Davies's in Wales, their first name was essential for proper identification.

Four days following admission, after a remarkable physical recovery, my wife was back on her feet (ably assisted by the physiotherapists at first).

Already, the physiotherapists had Margaret up and walking and now, every time I visited, we went for a short walk. Her colour returned and muscle tone quickly improved to almost normal. Margaret had only been off her feet a relatively short time and had suffered no muscle wastage as a direct result.

Although she was a bit shaky on her legs, there was no paralysis or other physical disability apparent. The physiotherapists had tried out

Margaret's limb functions on Tuesday. They then took her for a short walk by the process of grabbing an arm each and holding her up as they progressed along the corridor and back again.

Margaret had difficulty understanding how to move her left foot and her right, getting them wrong several times as she progressed down to the nurses station. Otherwise, she did just fine.

By now, Margaret was getting to know me as a trusted friend. We were starting to emulate the couple I saw on that first day. Margaret would become very animated and enthusiastic and smile and laugh a lot. She would try to tell me who had been in to see her each time I saw her, but her brain damage meant that she had not the words, or the names to help her.

Meanwhile, I was starting to feel the constant pressure. I was getting a bit ragged with having to cope with so many things. My brain was functioning on automatic and I was operating like the Fire Service, meeting each challenge as it occurred without any thought as to consequences or priority or order.

I was still only able to manage about six hours sleep each night.

My computer courses were still running. My business was still functioning. It was all happening. I needed a quick course in crisis management to be able to survive. At the ripe old age of sixty-seven, I did not think my body had been built for all that.

When I arrived home, the phone would be ringing. I would put the kettle on to make a welcome cup of tea. By the time I filled it with water, the phone would ring again. After the third or fourth attempt, I would make the tea but it was nearly cold before I could put it in a cup to drink.

I would eat my lunch sitting on the stairs, telling people what had happened and giving updates on progress. The Christmas cards had arrived at their destinations and Margaret's friends and relatives were all shocked that someone so vital and important in their lives had suffered an accident.

These people wanted all the news and any progress. I was required to be sincere and polite and concerned and informative while my brain was screaming at me to pull the plug and use the answer-phone.

But I knew that these were important anxious calls for Margaret's friends to make and I wanted to ensure that all their calls were answered. I owed it to Margaret and to them. So, I coped.

On one occasion, I fielded ten phone calls within the space of one hour and at the same time, I made my evening meal and a cup of tea. It is called progressive learning, I suppose.

I tried not to get flustered and took a leaf out of women's books by attempting something alien to the male gender – carrying out more than one task simultaneously. You know the sort of thing. Prop the phone up on your shoulder and carry on eating, or writing, or cooking, or whatever, whilst answering questions and doing updates.

By the third or fourth call, the answers were imprinted on my brain in any case. I used a lot of one-word sentences as well, careful to put the right weight and inflection on them to sound as if everything was going smoothly, that I was listening intently to their conversation and responding.

Of course, people offered to cook food, provide meals, do any washing, driving, shopping and all the things that they could think of to help. However, I knew that I would be needing that help later on and so asked for that rather than have the help at the time.

I wanted a free hand to structure my day even if it meant working long hours.

I have generally worked alone on projects and schemes throughout my life and this may have coloured my decision to continue unaided for the present at least. Someone else might have found the help people offered extremely valuable and even necessary.

On my hospital visits, I found that Margaret was difficult to understand in conversation. Her brain told her things that did not match up to what actually came out of her mouth.

At first, she ate her food as a left-handed person would with knife and fork transposed. She tried to eat soup with the spoon upside down. It was as if everything in her brain had been reversed.

She still referred to me as 'Him' and herself as 'Her'.

Imagine how difficult this is to comprehend by using these words in mock conversation with someone in place of words such as 'You' and 'Me'.

I could tell when Margaret was pleased with something I had done. She was ecstatic, almost over-reacting to things. Her inability to convey her meaning was both frustrating and hilarious.

My decision to allow visitors was paying off. Her friends were extremely tolerant and helped her to get back some of her conversational ability quite quickly. Have you seen how quickly a child of three picks up on adult conversation?

Well, it was of that order, or perhaps even faster.

The female visitors also helped my dear wife with other tasks such as a little walk, or a trip to the loo. I am aware that others in my situation have barred visitors completely and then expected everyone to act normally.

The human instinct for care and involvement in the healing process is huge. Just look at all the handholding that is done around the world by healing groups in times of stress or catastrophe. Some of those non-medical therapies really work, even if the effects are disputed.

Our Californian son, Neil, sent me an e-mail in response to my missive and wanted to know if he should travel over. I suggested that he wait until his scheduled trip over the 'Pond' for Christmas. His mother was apparently out of danger as far as anyone could tell and I would keep him posted of any developments. I knew that he would be worried sick about his lovely Mum whom he adored to bits.

By mid-week, I had settled into some sort of routine. I was still disorientated in the extreme. My head was still spinning with shock. Still six hours sleep at most, but what sleep. I could have slept for Wales, or for my home country – Scotland.

The pressure was on though and I was barely managing.

At least I had the washing under control. Put the powder in the slot at the top. Bung the clothes in the hole and shut the door. Select the program. Switch on and then go away to do something else. After tea, take the clothes out of the machine, press them flat by hand and peg them onto the line in the carport.

Every day, I hung up the washing either inside in the kitchen or, if it was dry, outside in the carport. I had recently kitted out the carport with clothes' lines for a rainy day and found it ideal. Funnily enough, Margaret had never opted to use this facility, but to me it was a boon.

To ensure that I never had to do any of this ironing stuff (that I recall from my army National Service days as being a bore), I used the 'minimum iron' setting on the washing machine as often as possible.

I folded things into the machine and then took them out of the machine as soon as it stopped its cycle. I smoothed them out into previous folds if they were big - like tablecloths and sheets, or just smoothed them out into their natural shape, something that produced nice-looking washing when it was dry.

My shirts, I hung out straight from the machine onto coat hangers – something I recalled from my sons in their university days!

Before going to bed, I would take in the washing and transfer it to the line in the kitchen above the heating duct. Then first thing in the morning, lay it all flat, smooth it out by hand and fold it into convenient sizes and piles. Put Margaret's stuff in the case and bingo – ready to go.

What do you mean, 'What about ironing?'

If we have an iron, I never found it. I never had time to look for it. Same is true for an ironing board, though I did know where that lived since I usually offered to put it away if I was around when Margaret was finished with it.

Somewhere in between, I fitted in my meals, my courses, my customers and most days, three visits each day to the hospital. I also managed some of the Christmas shopping when I had to go to the Bank either for the business or when I needed cash.

Next day, I had to miss the morning visit to the Hospital. That day's computer course was in Cowbridge – about sixteen miles down the M4 and then narrow lanes up to the old A48 and back in to the quaint country town with its cattle market still thriving. I made it back to the hospital in time for the next consultant appointment though.

That meeting with the Dr Olds was a revelation. The Consultant further described to me the injury in some detail, including the amount of obvious damage.

He gave me the reason why they could not operate to remove the clot that had formed. It was too deep within the brain and the resulting damage to get to the clot would only make matters worse. He hinted that Margaret was making a very good recovery but it was early days.

The clot, as far as I could tell from his description, was directly in line with the small abrasion I had seen on the left side of her head.

Geraint Olds then informed me that Margaret had made good progress and she would be moving on Friday to a rehabilitation unit.

This was indeed good news. She could now walk unaided if slowly to the loo and to have a wash as well, so things were really looking up.

There was still, however a major speech problem and some considerable, if not total loss of memory. For someone who relied on speech so much in her busy interesting - even exciting life, the knock-on effects were beyond comprehension.

Both the Church and the Floral Club were particularly badly hit due to the flu' epidemic and the usual pre-Christmas arrangements. Margaret was sorely missed in her normal helpful endeavours.

Later when I discussed Margaret with my doctor friend Chas, he confirmed everything that Margaret's Consultant had said about the possible prognosis for recovery.

Our Gloucestershire friends, Gerry and Monica had phoned to ask if they could visit, so I invited them on Thursday for a cold buffet lunch and escort to the hospital. They did not wish to add to my burdens but as relative strangers to the area, the offer to take them to see my wife clinched matters.

This couple has always been so kind and generous that I felt a cold meal (almost the height of my culinary powers) was the least I could do. There was cold ham and smoked salmon as well as a selection of cheeses and all the salady stuff.

Margaret's friend Monica deftly showed me how to 'dress' the green salad that I had prepared. My *'piece-de-resistance'* has always been setting the table and I believe that this is often the secret of a successful meal. The table looked splendid and a bottle of Chardonnay lay in the fridge, chilled and ready to serve in cut-glass stem glasses.

I needn't have bothered. They weren't drinking and driving. In fact the cheese attracted more attention than anything else. To my chagrin but to my credit, I sacrificed three pieces of the Ellen Rowe apple and blackberry pie —served with fresh cream - to finish off the meal before we all piled into my Mondeo for the visit.

I had worked out a plan to get free parking for my visits since the 'Pay and Display' parking cost £1.50 a time. My visits were never for more than an half-hour. Yet each day's parking would cost me £4.50 for the three visits, or over £30 in a week and I am Scottish, don't forget!

Margaret was surprised and delighted to see our friends from the Forest of Dean, but then she showed the same reaction to whoever came to see her. I had introduced so many people as her friends, or given their relationship status. Margaret therefore understood that the visitors were important in her life.

I formed the impression that this effusive welcome was a sort of safety tactic since Margaret was now aware that she should know *all* the people who came to visit. However, on this occasion, it perked her up and she was able to converse with them in a rather stilted uncomfortable way. I wondered if there had been any spark of recognition.

By this time, Margaret was looking a healthier colour - probably due to the solid food. Both Gerry and Monica separately remarked on her bright condition because I had described Margaret as she had been at the weekend when they had phoned in response to my insert in their Christmas card.

So she must be recovering.

The mass of flowers and the plants brightened her little corner of the ward and helped to lessen the diminished urine smell. I was pleased for their sakes that the ward now looked brighter.

Later that day, Margaret's close personal friend, Ellen Rowe (of the apple and blackberry pie) popped in to see her again and engaged her in conversation. During the flow of verbiage, my wife called her by her name - which was amazing since, up until then everyone had been, 'Him', or 'Her'.

Ellen Rowe was equally surprised at being called by her right name. She said to Margaret, 'And what's my name? Do you know who I am?'

Margaret was puzzled. 'Well, I know your face but I don't know your name! I don't know what you are called'.

This variation in memory recall is quite common according to the Speech Therapist I talked to about the phenomenon. It allows recall within conversation but prevents that process when the brain searches for individual words, or words not supported by others.

Even ten years post-accident, Margaret still exhibits this characteristic when she is interrupted in the middle of speech.

She cannot pick up the thread again and sometimes, she cannot even recall the bit of the conversation prior to the interruption.

Every day, mostly three times a day, I had collected washing, checked her needs, left notes or spoke to nursing staff about her problems. I then went home, put the washing in the machine, added the powder or liquid and switched on before making myself something to eat.

I caught a few naps throughout the day whenever I could - usually broken by the sound of the telephone. I mused again about pulling the plug, but I felt a keen sense of duty to be available whenever people phoned. Even with the phone calls, it was a lonely unhappy existence.

By Thursday of that second week, there were hints from the Registrar of a move in the offing for Margaret. The word 'rehab' kept cropping up in the conversation.

'Amazing recovery rate' was also a phrase used by the nurses on occasion. I didn't tell the Registrar about the earlier rehab. conversation with his boss. (It is called, 'Need-to-know!').

The following day, I visited Margaret at 8.30 am before my first class of the day and again at 3.30pm after my second two-hour class had ended. The date was Friday, December 3rd 1999 and outside there was a noticeably chill wind and some early ice on the roads.

My Friday early-afternoon trip to the Ward seemed to trigger everything. I bumped into Dr Olds who stopped me in my tracks. 'We're moving Mrs Greenridge today. I'll arrange it now'. And that was exactly what he did.

There right in front of me, he picked up the telephone and in a few short sentences and instructions, it was arranged. In minutes, all Margaret's gear - the flowers, fruit, clothes, mineral water bottles, cordial and all the cards were catalogued, packed and ready.

The ward staff had compiled a list of all her belongings and I was told that everything on the list had been checked and would be checked in by the receiving hospital at the other end.

She moved within the hour to the Cardiff Royal Infirmary's West Wing. This was the Stroke Unit and Rehabilitation Centre.

The establishment was some two miles away from the University Hospital on the edge of Cardiff's City Centre. I never imagined that such a short routine journey would cause any problems. But then, I forgot about Murphy's Law!

Chapter Three
Rehabilitation

The West Wing of Cardiff Royal Infirmary was a total change from the University Hospital. Margaret's friend Ellen Rowe told her that she gave birth to her youngest child on the second floor (B Floor) of the West Wing when it was a Maternity Unit.

The old Infirmary next door has all but closed since then. Meantime, the Maternity Unit had been converted into a Geriatric Rehabilitation Unit. So, in West Wing, instead of 'seeing them in' as helpless newborn babies, they now tend to 'see them out' as equally helpless geriatrics.

This amazing change of function happened several years ago and was masterminded by my friend and colleague, Professor John Pathy, (who specialized in stroke-therapy as a particular section of Geriatric Medicine). The building now houses amongst other things, the Stroke Unit - which was where Margaret had been sent.

This was a different type of health care unit to the University Hospital ward where Margaret had been admitted initially. For a start, there was not much of that smell of stale urine. Most patients had the dubious luxury of a room to themselves and ongoing therapy was a scheduled part of the daily activity.

The addition of the flowers, the plants and the bright 'Get Well' cards livened up the dullness of Margaret's room and made it all the more comfortable and homely. The nursing and ancillary staff eventually used up most of the vases and jars on C Floor for Margaret's flowers as they started to arrive from her many friends.

I brought in some redundant circular plastic margarine tops to put under the plants so that they could be watered without soiling everything else.

By that day, Margaret knew roughly who I was and could recognise me when I arrived with her changes of clothing and food extras.

Her speech was improving. Well, I suppose what I really mean is that her halting vocabulary was expanding. The constant round of visitors and their short visits gave her ample opportunity for picking up new words and phrases and the subject matter was always the same. You know – '*How are you? Are they feeding you?*' etc.

Margaret was very fit for her 65 years. She had always been active and always needed something to occupy her time. Probably her general fitness played an important part in her speedy physical recovery.

I arrived at the Royal Infirmary West Wing at about 6.30pm on that Friday evening. Margaret was firmly installed with all her things, including cards and flowers in her single room on the second floor.

She looked a bit cold and shivery although the room was pleasantly warm to me. She told me in halting words about her nightmare trip from the University Hospital, holding up a blanket every now and then and shaking her head to illustrate her story.

Most of her conversation started, '*And the ....*'.

The rest was a fireworks spectacular of hands waving in all directions, with pointing fingers at various angles. This to the accompaniment of strange words that had no real meaning for me.

This initial burst of energy was followed by another, '*And the ....*', with a repeat performance of the hand-waving plus more of the strange utterings.

The ambulance that took her from one hospital to the other was the type for transporting ambulant patients. More an open bus than a van, with big double doors at the back. Margaret was dressed in just her summer-weight light cotton nightdress and matching light cotton dressing gown with no coat or blanket. I suppose that these would be adequate for a centrally heated hospital ward and perhaps for mid-summer, but this was mid-December.

Every time the doors at the back of the ambulance were opened to let someone out, a blast of early evening arctic air blew in. There were no blankets obvious and Margaret froze.

The journey between the two hospitals should have taken no more than ten minutes, but some of the patients were going to out-of-town locations and West Wing at Cardiff Royal Infirmary was last on the driver's list on this bitter and, as it happened, coldest day of the year in 1999.

In the ambulance, Margaret sat huddled up in her nightdress to try to conserve her heat. The heating was on, of course, so the vehicle heated up between stops.

Well, it took about an hour for the journey and she was most unhappy. She was unable to tell the driver of her plight because she did not know the words.

I am sure the driver would have provided her with any number of blankets if he had realised her condition. However, he was blissfully ignorant of her plight. Communication difficulties were going to plague Margaret from now on.

Margaret was being transferred from one centrally heated hospital to another. And this ambulance crew were first line caring professionals! How could they miss the obvious? She managed to convey to me that the driver asked for directions at each port of call so perhaps he was new to the job.

The ambulance travelled all the way to the outskirts of Cardiff and to some of the suburbs on its frosty journey. Whatever these guys say about patient care, there was none of it evident on that journey into the cold December night. She might just as well have been a sack of potatoes for delivery to the hospital.

None of our family and friends, or I for that matter, imagined that the transfer of Margaret to the rehabilitation unit only two miles away would present with any problems. My usual check of Murphy's Laws missed that vital fifth law (*Even when nothing can go wrong, something will always go wrong*).

Hospitals did such transfers every day. Patients were transferred into and out of hospital as a matter of course. But not Margaret, it seems.

When such idiotic things occur, there are two courses of action open to one. The first is to create a big stink with the authorities that such inhuman acts are allowed to happen. The second is to try to think of some positive benefit that may have accrued.

I had no time for any aggravatory action, so I was forced to think of something good that may have come out of the incident. The only placatory idea that I had was the thought that, during the Korean War, injured soldiers and in particular those with head injuries, were often stretchered to the base hospital suspended under helicopters in the depth of that Korean winter.

It was noted that these casualties arrived in better condition than those transported within the relative warmth and safety of the helicopter cabin. But I suspect that this philosophy takes a bit of swallowing in Margaret's case.

On Saturday, I managed three visits.

Margaret felt a bit isolated being on her own for the first time since the accident. One of the benefits of a busy ward was that there was always something going on and people to communicate with. A single room lacked those advantages to someone in Margaret's condition. She really needed to be able to see people and to be reassured all the time. So, I was thankful for the friends who visited.

More cards and flowers arrived and the nurses provided more vases. They carefully stuck all the 'Get Well' cards on a board on the wall, or stood them up on the windowsill.

On my first visit, the place seemed familiar and then I recalled having visited the West Wing in my professional capacity several years ago when it was a Maternity Hospital. It was also noted for its great Christmas parties in those days.

When I had raided the fridge at the University Hospital to take any remaining yoghurts to the West Wing, I found that my paper-bag of goats milk yoghurts was still intact, as I had delivered it. None of the contents had been touched. Only the first individual small carton that I had taken in had been used in three days. I was not amused.

I immediately made sure that the appropriate staff on duty at the West Wing who did the teas and breakfasts were aware of the yoghurt. Sure enough, they did start straight away to provide it with Margaret's breakfast. But, they soon lapsed as time went by.

Margaret was starting to remember things now. She asked me about some gadget in the kitchen at home. It was the ward kitchen opposite her room that had helped her memory. She kept pointing to the kitchen and her ears.

I deduced correctly that it was her little radio only because I knew that she liked to listen to Radio 4 every day.

When I brought it in, it had to be checked by the hospital electrician before being plugged into the mains but it passed their testing easily enough.

This set me thinking of things to keep her amused between therapy sessions and visitors.

When she showed me a magazine she had 'read', it appeared that the only bits that she looked at were the pictures, so my brain said 'Telly'. I said that I would bring her in a TV next time.

Before leaving the unit, I checked with the ward staff and they said that it would be alright to do this.

The portable TV from our bedroom stood comfortably on the top of her wardrobe locker to one side of the hospital room and the cable just reached the socket on the wall. Reception was good on five of the nine channels.

I thought that was the end of it until Margaret asked me what to do with the tele-pilot. She could not grasp what the numbers represented. I showed her that pressing each one in turn changed the channel, or alternatively, she could use the channel changer below the numbers.

Very much confused, she agreed to try it. She seemed to understand the volume control best of all. Funnily enough, even today, she has trouble using a tele-pilot.

It took her a couple of days to get used to the TV. Then the significance of lying in bed to view the pictures dawned on her and she started to use it quite sensibly, though often she would turn down the sound and just watch the pictures.

I drew pictures of the digits on the clock on the radio to indicate what time to switch on for her favourite programs, thinking that I was being helpful. Margaret failed to understand their significance. It was all too high-powered for her to understand. But, in her own little way, she seemed to like the fact that I was doing things to make her life more pleasant.

Next day being Sunday, I took the opportunity to place an update card in the foyer of the Church on my normal Sunday attendance. It described what had happened and indicated that Margaret was making good progress. In order to fend off phone calls, I included the change of hospital and ward details.

Once again, it took me a while to get out at the end of the Sunday Service. Everyone seemingly wanted the up-to-date news of Margaret and her progress directly from me rather than on a piece of card.

One or two people had turned up at the University Hospital asking for Margaret on the previous Saturday unfortunately. There is a bus from that hospital into town but by the time you actually arrive at the University Hospital for evening visiting it is too late to make the second journey to the Rehab. Unit at the Cardiff Royal.

I had let some of Margaret's friends know on Friday that Margaret was on the move but there is no quick way of distributing such information. Not everyone has e-mail and phoning is too time-consuming since everyone feels that they need to chat about the accident.

Now, people were dropping in every day to see Margaret and bringing fruit or flowers or chocolates. This was beneficial in many ways to Margaret's recovery. It was something for which I shall always feel eternally grateful to those who undertook this very valuable service.

Some people from the Church failed to see my notice about the change of hospital and ward and took two buses each way to the University Hospital when one would have taken them past the Infirmary.

I apologised to them when they phoned, thanking them profusely. I realised only too well the significance of the long and involved, though wasted journey these elderly people had made just for the chance to see their much-loved Margaret.

Visitors came from further a-field. Our friends, the Roberts family came all the way from Plymouth. I invited them to lunch and set the dining room for a cold buffet lunch once again. Why move the goal posts, I thought? It worked well last time we had visitors who came from a distance to see Margaret in hospital.

Out came the same cold lunch scenario, as on the last time I had to cater for visitors. The salad dressing made on the previous occasion was still in the fridge and one of the visitors found it, tasted it and declared it about the best she had ever tasted. There was fresh cold ham off the bone, smoked salmon and some nice fresh bread.

I slipped up on the Flora margarine though. There had been some potatoes left over from my main meal on the previous day. (Quite a few times I had made enough for two as I usually did before the accident). I thought of slicing and frying these as part of my next meal. The potatoes were stored in an empty Flora carton and I had put them in the fridge.

Needless to say, it was these that landed on the table for lunch instead of the real carton of spread. When it was opened in mistake for the real Flora, it raised the tone of lunch quite a lot, so it wasn't really a disaster.

These people had travelled about 160 miles and did the return trip on the same day. As firm family friends, the Roberts date back to our Plymouth days when our two boys were born. They lived directly opposite us across the road in those far off days.

Happy days!

Their visit - all the way from Devon - was another enormous morale booster and a jolt for Margaret's memory. These were almost family - certainly adopted family if there is such a thing. We have some lovely friends.

I had noticed that there were some sheets of paper on the small table in Margaret's room when I arrived with the TV. One of the therapists had been getting Margaret to draw the shapes of three or four capital letters of the alphabet. Margaret had no idea what she was doing. She was just copying the shapes.

I could hardly believe what was going on since I knew nothing of the therapy given to stroke patients. As far as I was concerned, Margaret knew all about letters and was a whiz with figures and forms and schedules.

It was inconceivable that she could not recognise letters. I asked her about them. She pointed to the pen and pencil and just indicated that she had been asked to draw the shapes. She could not remember why, but it was good.

That night I had a dream in Technicolor. I hardly ever dream and then usually in black and white.

When we went to Beijing a few years ago, we visited a Peking Duck restaurant as part of our tour. I was wearing a jersey-wool sweater in expectation of a sudden drop in the evening temperature.

The temperature however, remained high throughout the evening, so the jersey looked a bit out of place in the heat of the Beijing night. It caught the eye of the restaurant waiter who thought I looked cold and would bring me something to warm me up.

This turned out to be wild mushrooms. They tasted peculiar so I ate only one of them. That night too, I dreamed in full colour. I was so hot that I slept on top of the covers.

To get back to this dream in my own bed in my own house, someone (God? Or was it something I had seen and heard on TV?) was explaining to me that Margaret was incapable of calling up what were apparently code-pages of individual letters of the alphabet. (Ah, it must be a talking computer. They use 'Code Pages' to recall alphabetical letters!).

There was an illustration of the way in which the mind instantly recalls these code-pages as prompts for each letter - usually in response to their initial sound - such as 'ay' or 'bee' rather than 'ah' or 'buh' - reaching the brain. The illustration used two ancient-looking letters of the alphabet that floated around like kites until they were firmly anchored into place at the beginning of each word.

I assumed later that this phenomenon applied only to the initial letters of words after studying the way in which Margaret tried to recall letters to begin a word. Below, I have drawn the two example letters used in my dream out of interest.

There were only ever the two letters in the illustration/dream as shown above.

There is a copy of 'The Book of Kells' in our bookcase, but the illustrated letters in that tome are entirely different to the ones in my dream. I checked just to make sure.

In my dream, these two letters 'A' and 'B' roamed around as if they were lost until the found their niche and then anchored themselves into place.

This part of the dream gave me a clue as to part of Margaret's speech problem. I discovered that if I prompted her with the initial letter, then she could recall the word she wanted. Though this method was certainly not foolproof by any means. I would often have to try several letters before Margaret said the word she was looking for.

It suddenly came to me that Margaret could have lost the first letter of every word from her brain's vocabulary. Or perhaps her problem had something to do with the alphabetical sequencing. Then I went back into my usual deep sleep.

When I woke in the morning, I hastily wrote down the two letters as near to the design as I could recall. Sadly, the grey-scale colours used in the picture above cannot do full justice to the bright reds and yellows of my dream.

However, the overall impression given by the letters is about right. Both were in some ancient archaic style and in an archive of letters. The sort of thing you see in an illustrated Bible or old manuscript. Perhaps they were hanging flags such as one sees hung from a Bandsman's trumpet, or in a church that hosts a Services Memorial Chapel.

I must reiterate that I hardly ever dream and then, as I have indicated, usually in black and white. I have never been able to recall anything from my dreams before, so this was most surprising. Because I had hardly ever recalled what I dream, I have placed some particular significance on this occurrence.

Later events indicated that there was some validity in the hypothesis from the point of view of Margaret's retraining. Although, I must admit that I did not fully implement this hypothesis due to other pressures. I have however, used individual parts of the dream (as much as I can recall) with some measure of success.

Life is very strange at times.

The next week was easier.

My contract courses were coming to an end for the season so there was more time to plan each day, do the shopping, the washing and the visits.

I was able to think a bit more about the future. The rest of the Christmas cards were finished off and the little notes inside sparked off another reign of terror from the dreaded telephone calls. If only there were more people on e-mail!

If I say that I coped well with the phone calls, then I mean that there were no tears - only gentle words describing what had happened and how Margaret was progressing. All the time, I was screaming inside for some relief from it all, but my health service experience of working alone and under intense pressure 'On Call' proved an invaluable aid to coping.

While in Church Street one day I took the opportunity to take a few more photographs of the uneven paving and persuaded an interested bystander to waggle one of the paving blocks with his foot for the video camera.

The guy wanted payment until I explained what I was doing. Then he was a great help in selecting blocks to film. No level playing field this. Plenty of traps and trips for the unwary here - some as much as three inches deep and full of black water.

On the third day at West Wing, Margaret's speech had improved a bit and she was able to tell me that she had enjoyed the yoghurt. But there was still something missing from her breakfast. I carefully went through her usual foods and after a bit of brain coaxing (mine), I came up with apple juice.

Margaret laughed joyously and clapped this effort because I had tried really hard to understand her twirling hands and signs without any success. It was just a flash of inspiration.

The table in her room had more sheets of paper on it with some child-like drawings and a few more examples of letters. The therapists were starting Margaret on the road to recovery of her reading ability. Starting from scratch with forming the letters of the alphabet gave a good indication of the amount of lost brain cells.

The day after taking in the apple juice, Margaret showed me a little drawing she had made of a carton with a pouring spout to indicate to the maid who served breakfast that she wanted her apple juice to pour over her cornflakes. She was informed that there was no juice - an answer that puzzled her a lot. So there was still trouble for Margaret in getting the goodies I had so carefully replenished in the ward kitchen fridge across the corridor.

When I staggered in later in the day, she showed me the drawing again and said that she had not had any of that. I took her by the hand and showed her the big carton of apple juice on the shelf in the kitchen fridge beside her yoghurts.

The yoghurts were going down and Margaret told me that she was having them every day now. This inspired another notice to the staff about the apple juice. Margaret always used it instead of milk to pour over her cornflakes because of her lactose intolerance. Cows milk and dairy products abound with lactose.

Margaret's room was gradually filling up with flowers and cards.

She was still having daily physiotherapy for her limbs and speech therapy both for talking and for comprehension. There was also some psychological stuff (that she didn't understand) and of course, good nursing care.

Soon Margaret could copy her name in block capitals even though she could not really understand the meaning. This was evidenced when I took in our digital travel clock. She asked me what it was for, but did not understand the numbers or what they represented in terms of time.

She asked me about the 'day'. Margaret did not understand how it all worked. When did she get fed? And when did she have to go to sleep?

These were puzzling questions for her.

When I got home from that visit, I sat down at my computer and devised a schematic representation of a typical day-clock, based on the sun's movement. It was basically an arc drawn across a page in landscape. On it, I devised a chart of hospital events from sunrise to sunset.

These were linked to getting out of bed in the morning up until going to bed at night. I plotted key times across the sun's progress in digital style and added pictures of cups of tea and plated meals at mealtimes and a schematic bed at the beginning and end of the arc. (See opposite).

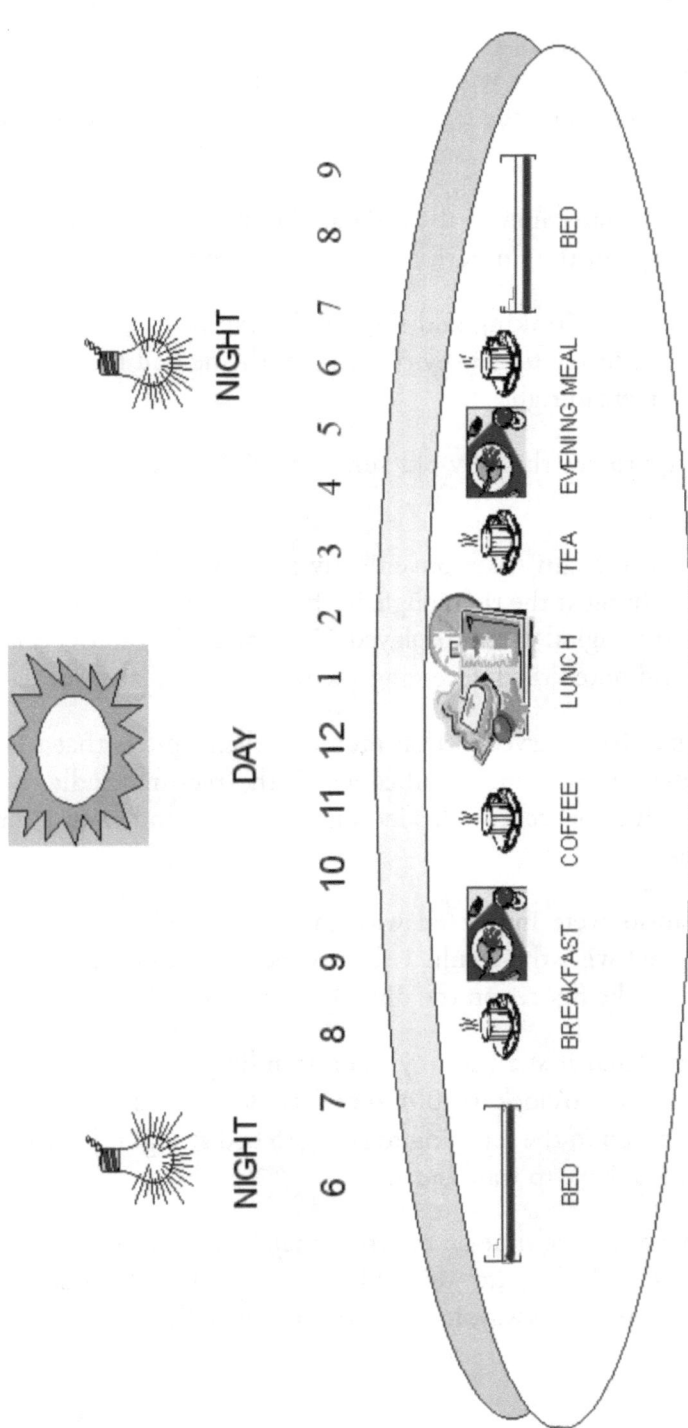

Along the perimeter of the arc, the sun was placed strategically as if it was in the sky. The arc was coloured darkening blue from the middle outwards to illustrate the transition from night to day and thence day to night.

I showed Margaret how it all worked, altering the digits on the clock and pointing out the similarity to the figures on the paper.

I mimed eating, drinking and sleeping in line with the items arrayed along the arc to try to convey the general theme and the order of the events from left to right.

Outside her room, the jolly old sun was shining out of a bright blue sky.

I pointed to the sun that conveniently and coincidentally, because it was winter, hung at the right angle in the sky, lighting her south-facing window. The digital clock displayed 12:00 and Margaret checked the diagram and noted the figures and the picture of a plated meal.

If lunch had been served at that moment, then I guess that Margaret would have grasped the significance of the picture. Sadly, hospital mealtimes did not seem to depend on my artistic endeavours for their timetables.

The therapists were impressed with my efforts and Margaret looked really pleased with the result. I showed her how to check the digital time against the figures on the digital clock-radio.

Still, I wondered if she had any understanding of the progress of the digits from seven o'clock (07:00) to twenty-one o'clock (21:00). That is, from getting up in the morning to going to bed at night. I decided that we would just have to wait and see.

The Arabic figures of time on my chart matched the shape of the digital figures on the clock quite well and after a couple of days she got the message, I think. Anyway, it solved one problem for her.

One of the dilemmas I later came across was that Margaret did not only misunderstand figures, she was still unsure about left and right. How do you cure that?

The little table in the room was soon littered with Margaret's attempts to write her own name on the paper provided. The letters were about two inches high and a bit scrawny but you could see the word 'MARGARET' in there somewhere.

Soon, Margaret was able to copy the lower case (small) letters for her address. She was beginning to grasp the significance of the capital letters that she used for her name and to associate sounds with the letters. The lower case letters meant nothing though.

She had no comprehension of what 'address' meant and therefore gave it low priority for learning. That was when I thought about the children's alphabet books and the 'First Dictionary' that I had bought with the twins in mind for Christmas.

On one of my Christmas shopping expeditions, I had called into the bookshop in Church Street. There were some little starter booklets of numbers and letters for young children. I bought one of each before I noticed the lovely illustrated children's dictionary and added that to my haul.

These three books were intended for our three-year-old twin grandchildren when they came to visit. After I had the dream about the letters 'A' and 'B', I thought that these might be useful for Margaret to look at during the day. Memory being what it is when you get older, I had forgotten all about the books until Margaret's work-sheets triggered the thought again.

Surprisingly, the large A4 size dictionary with its illustrations proved more popular with her than the smaller, simpler ABC and 123 books. But then life was full of surprises in those early days of rehabilitation.

On one evening, I slumped into one of the lounge chairs at home and switched on the TV. One of those old Black and White films had just started, so I didn't catch the title.

The film was about a lady in the US who suffered a stroke for some reason. The leading lady was none other than Glenda Jackson, so I watched and occasionally dozed.

As the plot unfolded, I realized that it was a film that was very pertinent to my situation. It was called '*The Patricia Neal Story*' after the book by Roald Dahl, her husband.

The author had enlisted the help of all the village neighbours to rehabilitate his wife. This was in the absence of any support services for stroke patients at that time in the US but partly due to distance from hospital amongst other things. The hypothesis sounded reasonable, so I made a mental note to follow that example in Margaret's case if the situation merited it.

As the days passed, whenever I visited the hospital, Margaret would show me the results of her latest therapy sessions.

I recall the day I went in to see her and she shook my arm excitedly and pointed to her bed. 'I did that myself', she said proudly. 'I got the lady to show me how to make the bed and then I did it on my own'.

It was not the time to be amused or disdainful. These new achievements represented huge strides in logic and understanding for her. What courage and determination she must have had to master the sequence of actions necessary to make her own bed! The grandchildren can do it today but they are twelve years old now and have the benefit of watching mummy do it every day for all those years.

My sister arrived again from Boston in Lincolnshire and stayed a few days. She was a great help with meals and things, releasing me to attend my courses and answer the phone.

She frowned on my way of dealing with the ironing. With hindsight, she realised that it was sufficient for the things that would be worn for a day and would then need re-washing such as underwear and nighties.

It is over two hundred miles from Boston to Cardiff and so she stayed overnight in the twin-bedded room that we call the 'Blue Room' for the colour scheme.

She was pleased to see that Margaret was improving. The two had a common interest in music and opera and regularly attended the Cardiff Singer of the World Competition together and also the Leeds International Piano Competition.

My taste in music was different, favouring the tunes from the fifties and sixties that occasionally have a stab at a comeback, and then retire into the archives again. Neither of us goes for this tuneless unintelligible modern stuff that echoes from every Ghetto Blaster, it seems.

Meanwhile, Margaret's room at the hospital looked more like a flower shop than part of a hospital. The windowsill and the walls were covered in over 100 'Get Well' cards. There was an accumulation of bits of paper with Margaret's carefully-drawn letters on them.

Each day, her diet was improving.

It took over a week to beat the system and to train Margaret to ask for her supplies of yoghurt and apple juice for breakfast. But then meals come from a central source and there is not much control over them once the dietician has made a list of what you need for each meal. It all happens automatically.

However individual the staff might try to make it, supplying meals for everyone has to be automated to a degree rather than specifically tailored to each patient. Many of the Stroke victims couldn't tell the difference until their brain recovers, so I guess that it was not a high-priority issue.

As far as I could tell, the staff all knew about Margaret's lactose intolerance and produced food accordingly. I continued to supply her yoghurt and apple juice. Margaret became accustomed to getting it from the communal fridge in the kitchen across the way, where she could keep it until she needed it if the staff forgot. However, I suspect that others sampled the apple juice because it, unlike the yoghurt, quickly disappeared.

The Occupational Therapists and Physiotherapists continued to rehabilitate Margaret until her walking had improved almost to unaided. There was still that left/right mix-up problem with her feet though.

It took only a few days of this attention before Margaret could recognise some of the letters of the alphabet and could write her given name at least. So the treatment was working. Her writing was a bit large for normal use but it was a start. Margaret was later taught to make herself a cup of tea in the kitchen annex wherein was the fridge with the yoghurt and apple-juice.

Christmas was in the offing, so I asked to see the Consultant again to discuss the future. There seemed no reason for Margaret to spend Christmas in hospital. We had previously arranged to have Christmas with our elder son and his family.

We had also booked a three-day holiday in Bournemouth that I would have to cancel and lose the deposit (my Scottish instincts forebade such a thought) if we could not make it. The break would give us a chance to try out Margaret's newfound skills.

Dr Olds thought that Margaret would be ready for discharge on, or not long after the 22nd of December 1999. I suggested that we might compromise a bit on the date if I took responsibility for Margaret to leave on Friday 17th.

The time was necessary in my view, to give Margaret a chance to acclimatise to the outside world again before heading off for Christmas. Although Dr Olds was not too happy about the situation, he agreed to look at Margaret's progress with my idea in mind.

During Margaret's first week at the rehabilitation centre, all my computer courses came to an end. There were a few private visits to do but I had declined any new work and so I would be free from 12th December. That would give me a few days to prepare for Margaret coming home and also to tie up the Christmas loose ends.

I had suggested that Margaret be trained to use the stairs so that she could go to bed normally at home. Despite the proximity of a nice wide staircase, this never materialised for some inexplicable reason.

On my evening hospital visits, Margaret and I had taken to having a short walk along the corridor and round into the next short corridor. There was a view from the end window over the eastern part of Cardiff's Adamsdown district at night – not a pretty sight at anytime but much better at night.

The hotel on the opposite side of the road sported a neon sign. Margaret became interested in it and asked me what it said since she could not read the words. I told her it said 'SPLOTTLANDS HOTEL'. It was hilarious – Margaret tried all ways to get her tongue round the two words.

'Shloplands' was the nearest she could manage after several tries. I realised it was quite a mouthful and while I joined in her mirth, I decided that this was a challenge that she must conquer. I hope the landlord of the hotel never finds out.

Each night after that, we would walk along to see the sign. Margaret would try very hard to say, 'SPLOTTLANDS' without success. After about three or four nights she was suddenly successful and I could see the effect that it had on her. She was elated and proud of her achievement.

This was an important break-through in learning. It was a first step towards reading and understanding. It still brings tears to my eyes just to recall that moment of triumph.

It was round about that time that Margaret suddenly recalled her shopping visit on that fateful day of the accident.

She struggled to tell me about her purchase of the sewing box in Howells. She tried to describe it to me and where she had bought it but she was so excited and animated that I had to calm her down in order to understand her.

It was only when she said the first part of the name of our daughter-in-law Jennifer, that I realised what she was on about.

Up until then I was completely mystified. Being male and lacking women's intuition, this was to become a fairly common occurrence.

I went into Howells Department Store after I raided Margaret's handbag at home to find the Bill. I was lucky to find the actual shop assistant who had served Margaret. She had the box wrapped and I humped it halfway across town to where I had parked the car. Fortunately, my experience of humping computers around the country came in handy for someone of my age and infirmity.

Margaret was pleased when I told her that I had retrieved the Christmas present. This proved to be the first pertinent piece of immediate post-accident memory to return to her damaged brain.

We tried some more with the books I had bought for the children. Margaret's various therapy sessions were going well and her mind started to pick things up just like a child's. Unfortunately, she still had difficulty recalling what she had learned and so on each visit, I quickly remembered to start all over again at the beginning on each occasion.

The repetitive nature of these visits paid off and gradually there were signs that she was taking some of it in. I doubt if I would have had the courage to start if I had realised that it would take Margaret at least one whole year to master the alphabet and then only on a good day.

I was still concerned about the stairs. Nothing had been done to teach Margaret and so I tried her on the stairs between the floors in the hospital on most visits. She managed quite well after a few abortive attempts but would only try out her new skill when she was holding tightly to my arm. That right/left foot problem persisted.

With computer courses finished and little or no private work coming in, I had more time to adjust to the prospect of Margaret returning home and thought that I could probably get by.

On the Saturday I called into the local Church Christmas Fair and bought a couple of apple tarts and put them in the freezer. Our very dear friend Ellen Rowe, had also given me another one of her glorious home-baked apple pies the same day so I had a piece of it with my evening meal of Victoria fish and chips.

Of course I tested my culinary skills to the full by making some custard to go with the apple tart and poured some fresh cream over the top for good measure. (Victoria was at that time our almost local and favourite award-winning Fish & Chip Emporium).

Whilst I accepted that it was up to me to provide accommodation and food for family visitors and close friends who travelled long journeys from as far away as Plymouth and Boston, Lincs, there were other visitors and concerned neighbours who needed snacks and cups of tea - of which there were more than a few.

Normally, this would not have been too much of a problem but by now, my life and life-style had been totally disrupted by the accident as you might already have suspected, or if you have experienced similar problems. Yet my major concern was for Margaret's condition above all else.

The family came down from Reading on Saturday again. They had planned to travel down the M4 on the evening previous, but the twins had flu' and were coughing and spluttering too badly to travel. As with many childhood diseases, they had recovered and were of course nicely contagious next day - as you will see - when they arrived, with just the odd cough and snivel to show their lethal potential.

My son and I went in to see his Mum on our own. He had flown in from Germany on the Friday and had not been exposed to the bug. The twins Mum, Jenny was in the early throes of a cold or flu' and thought Margaret had enough to cope with without adding her woes or bugs. It was a good weekend for me because I revelled in having the twins more or less to myself.

The bug started to bite their Mum so the family wisely left early on Sunday and I set about clearing the rooms for whoever came next. I could now cope with the washing since I was doing at least once-daily loads using my by now, regular protocol.

On Sunday morning, I did a further update on Margaret's progress for our Church. I'm afraid there was a lot of coughing and spluttering going on at the Church that I totally ignored as I did by accepting the obligatory peck-on-the-cheek, 'mm-wah, mm-wah', from some of Margaret's more sympathetic friends.

With all this exposure to bugs and my two-a-day or three-a-day visits to the hospital, I might have expected some trouble in my weakened state. However, when it came, it hit me like a bomb.

It was not until Tuesday that I regretted my error in entertaining the twins at the weekend. I could hardly get up out of bed.

I telephoned my Tuesday client and for the first time in the twelve-year history of my business, I had to cancel.

This in itself made me feel bad, but I had contracted the real dreaded lurgy - the flu' that was to become epidemic throughout the Country during the Christmas period and beyond into January in the Millennium year.

I myself, who am almost never ill and a stranger to my GP, had contracted flu'!

What a disaster.

I, who never visit doctors or surgeries and survive each year on a total medication of perhaps six aspirins if that. I probably caught it from my adorable twin grandchildren on their second visit when their family came to see *'Grandma in ho'pital'* as the twins liked to chant. But then it could have been that visit to Church on Sunday.

I had the flu' for a total of two weeks and it took a further week to recover fully. During this time I still kept up the visits to my wife in hospital at least twice and often three times a day (keeping well away from her in the process).

I managed to keep up with the washing and drying, made my meals and answered the phone (a chore that kept me on my toes since I still had to sound cheerful and positive). Also, I needed to thank callers for their cards, flowers and hospital visits and their concern.

Meanwhile, I did the shopping as necessary and kept the house clean and tidy for the visitors (some of whom stayed the night and were fed and watered, as they say).

Every day was a challenge as the flu' bug bit deeper and deeper into my reserves of strength. Nevertheless, I continued with those vital hospital visits by living on eight-hour aspirins three times a day (equals twenty-four hours for the non-mathematical).

I was careful not to stay on my visits. Just change the clothing, drop the Christmas mail and give any messages. It was still an eighteen-hour day but with collapsing breaks built-in. Hey, I was nearly seventy at the time!

Margaret understood that I was ill and advised me to go home to bed and rest on every visit. She could see me getting worse.

It was on that day that I discovered that she was yet again not getting anything with her cornflakes even though I had alerted the nursing staff to the problem on regular occasions. So, eventually I put up another notice that there was goats' yoghurt in the fridge.

The tragedy was that Margaret knew where it was but still did not know how to convey the message to the maids or nurses when they changed shifts. She was always a bit scared of taking it from the kitchen despite my having shown her where it was kept.

Fortunately, the situation at home was all under control. I put my dirty clothes in the bathroom basket as usual and wiped round the sink and shower - all things well within my ability from previous training sessions long ago as part of ongoing preparation for married bliss. (Hers, or mine? I am not too sure for whom it was intended).

An added bonus was the well-stocked fridge, cupboards and freezer. Also, there were enough shirts, socks and underwear to last me a month at least. All I had to do was organise things in advance and do the odd bit of shopping for milk and bread - that I was accustomed to doing anyway.

It was, however a lonely celibate existence. I am not used to being ill. With no wife to support me and offer me some TLC, I was a lost soul in a sea of damp paper hankies.

Phone calls were a nightmare.

There were so many to deal with and remember to give all that repetitive explanation about what had happened to Margaret to all her dear friends and strangers alike. These calls inevitably produced a fair amount of water from my eyes, which proved to be a nuisance because it got into my glasses. Since I usually sat on the stairs, it occasionally fell down onto other, more embarrassing places. (I never cried of course).

Every day, despite my flagging spirits, I could see improvements. Margaret was excited by the newness of her every conquest - like a child finding out how to use a new toy. She was great and she was concerned for my health.

I took care not to get too near to her - something that paid off handsomely since she did not ever contract my flu'. She did have a sore throat and a few snivels but I took that as being due to the air-conditioning, or a local cold bug. She eventually got the hang of the TV pilot and could now also tune in the radio after I showed her the controls a few times.

I struggled in for three days to replace linen and keep the yoghurt and apple juice topped up. Margaret was once again receiving the breakfast additives and these made for a more enjoyable life.

By now, even all the vases from the ward below had migrated to Margaret's room to house the flowers as they arrived. The place looked like a film star's dressing room. I counted one hundred and ten cards on the wall and there were more along the back of the windowsill.

There were also plants in pots, sweets and chocolates, soft drinks, food parcels and face-wipes and magazines. I still kept out of Margaret's way just to make sure that she did not succumb to my bout of 'flu. Walks along the corridor were out, sad to say.

On the fourth day of the 'flu, my visits to hospital came to an end. Due to my persistence, the Team and the Consultant had agreed that Margaret could come out of hospital.

There must have been some fraught discussions because the Team wanted her for at least another two weeks. With hindsight, they were right in one sense in that we might have had some follow-up therapy sessions at home if I had kept to their schedule.

Geraint Olds had agreed to discharge Margaret into my care on Friday, 17 December and I dutifully collected her and her belongings somehow from the West Wing.

I know it was approaching Christmas with a huge flu' epidemic waiting in the wings but what happened after discharge from hospital was an appalling condemnation of the system as far as I was concerned as a novice Carer.

As time went on, I soon realized that the follow-up outpatient services usually available to stroke patients leaving hospital had been non-existent for Margaret. There was not even the mandatory home-visit just to check that she was still progressing and that we were able to cope on our own.

Perhaps my decision to take early responsibility for Margaret had interfered with the normal patient discharge system. I don't really think so, though. I consider that it was due to the proximity of Christmas, the ubiquitous administrative errors and the dreaded flu' epidemic.

Fortunately, the Hospital Team were proved wrong in thinking that we might have difficulty in surviving. But there should have been some follow-up. It was in the medical notes.

Margaret had asked me to arrange a hair appointment for the following Tuesday. The house was stocked up with food and there was nothing much left for me to do. The journeys to hospital had stopped and the telephone calls had diminished.

Margaret took a good long look around the house with me to check that she knew where everything was and I realised that perhaps some memory of old was stirring.

Think of the white settler in the cowboy era, who takes his new 'first nation' bride to his wooden shack (home) and shows her a kitchen of sorts, living rooms with furniture, a pile of bedding and a bed. For someone brought up in a teepee tent to sleep on the ground, or on an animal skin, there would be no comprehension of it all. Everything would be strange at first.

Margaret's knowledge of living space was limited to being in one room in a hospital environment. Food appeared at mealtimes and visitors arrived spasmodically throughout the day. She had lost all the household skill memories and would have to relearn to do everything, however trivial or simple to us comparative geniuses.

My difficulty was in realizing this and continually remembering to make allowances for that *all the time.*

We had one shot at trying the stairs and, with a bit of difficulty, Margaret could manage well enough on her own.

Her speech and memory had improved over those first three weeks to the stage where there were gaps that only serious ongoing training and time would complete.

Already she had been sorely missed in her various capacities. At the time, I thought that it would probably take six months or more for her to get back to some kind of normality. How wrong can you get?

Geraint Olds, her Consultant, had later given her a prognosis of three years in total to a more or less full recovery as far as she could go. He suggested a figure of about 90-95% of her pre- accident capability in that time.

While I totally misunderstood the inference, (about the effect of the missing 5-10%), I must admit that I personally doubted that she would ever get back that glow that marked her as a special person for so many people in her life.

Our evening meal we made together and then both went to separate beds. I said that I would sleep in the middle room so that Margaret would avoid too close contact. I would be near enough to hear her if she wanted anything, or woke up disorientated. I was distinctly worried about what would happen to her if she caught my fever. Her time in the hospital had adjusted her to sleeping on her own in any case.

One of the most important medicines that I obtained for her was that visit to the hairdresser on the following Tuesday. On that day, I crawled out of bed wondering how it would go. Margaret's first outing, where she would have to talk and respond to someone who was neither family, friend, nor hospital staff.

As expected, the trip cheered her up tremendously. The lank grey hair was washed and set and Margaret looked more her old self.

She felt better - particularly after a look in the mirror - and she had a good day. There was still that rather telling glaze to her eyes. I knew that we still had a long way to go to get back some of the old Margaret.

With the confidence inspired by the success of that outing to the hairdresser, we did shopping and walking regularly.

After a while, Margaret 'insisted' on us planning our day and our meals in advance so that she knew what we were doing each day. She also started to do her diary and household accounts again, even though she just wrote things randomly in her diary and copied the figures from the bill totals into a list.

She had no idea how to add up the totals.

My dearly beloved used a slim diary for events and an A5 page-a-day for accounts and household things. I would transfer the day's events to the household diary so that I had only one diary to consult.

Next morning, I could not get up out of bed. I had had it, so to speak. Margaret, on the other hand was able to change into day clothes and have her breakfast as usual.

It struck me that we had no back-up plan for such an eventuality. With me incapacitated, Margaret was in a pickle. I guess that in similar scenarios, some elderly couples just died and nobody could understand what happened.

We hear of such tales when they are splashed all over the media. You know the sort of thing. *'Police break into house after neighbour raises the alarm. Elderly couple found dead!'*

It doesn't really bear thinking about.

In our case, our ministering angel had already spread its wings and flew in all the way from Southern California. How fortunate we were.

With no one to guide her, Margaret was wondering what to do with herself when she heard a car draw up outside. It was December 22nd 1999 – some four weeks after the accident. Margaret was looking out of the lounge window and suddenly started shouting up to me, 'Neil, Neil. Neil's home!'

Our youngest son had flown in from San Francisco.

We were all trying to spend Christmas with the twins who live in Reading, but he had driven down to Cardiff from Heathrow directly he landed to see his Mum. It was exciting to realise that Margaret had recognised her younger son whom she had not seen for nearly six months.

Neil had been ready to fly over from day one of the accident. Thanks to e-mail, I had managed to reassure him as to his Mum's condition and the prognosis for the future. Even so, he had been prepared to give up his job at one stage just to be able to come home to see Mum and to express his love and concern.

He had hired a car at Heathrow following his long flight over the 'Pond' and drove straight down to Wales. I was amazed that Margaret had so easily recognised our son.

Neil assumed that his Mum must have recovered since he did not expect to find her at home.

Margaret told him that I was ill in bed and he came up with his airline carry-on bag. Said, '*Hi, Dad. Mum says you are not well. Have some of this*'.

My son had arrived with the bag of medicines that he always carried with him on his travels in order maintain his health during key times with his work.

His first action was to dose me up with what I can only describe as 'jollop' and pills containing everything but arsenic. He popped a couple of squirts of Echinacia into my mouth and then clamped my mouth shut so that I had no choice but to swallow the awful-tasting stuff.

Within the hour, I felt much better and by lunchtime I was back in the land of the living. It was really amazing.

I was still a bit weak when I got up, but I had a shower and came downstairs to have some lunch.

As the day progressed, I was almost back to normal. This was a timely recovery for we had planned to pop along the M4 to our eldest son's house in Reading to celebrate Christmas.

There had been a thin covering of snow overnight but by midday it had disappeared. What a cool welcome for Neil after the warmth of California most of the year round.

Neil had planned to spend Christmas Day and Boxing Day with his brother and family and then go off skiing in the Alps. We were all set to cancel our projected trip to Bournemouth from 27th-29th December but I realised that our plans fitted his plans perfectly. So we still had a 'Go' on that trip.

Since coming home from hospital, I had continued with Margaret's speech and memory training using some of the material from the Hospital Rehab.Unit.

Sadly, my Computer Software Training business had suffered badly since I was unable to take on any new work or seek new contracts because of the accident. There was no one else available to look after the general running of the house and to provide essential food and clean clothing for my dear wife.

No Social Services back-up. Nothing!

Utilising the two books of alphabet and numbers that I had purchased for our twin grandchildren, I had started some daily retraining exercises for Margaret.

I would make a cup of tea at seven o'clock every morning. Then we would spend about an hour and a half each morning on those 'Children's' books before going down to breakfast.

During this time I would go over what she had done in the hospital. Then it was mainly looking at the letters and numbers and their accompanying pictures in the books I had bought for the grandchildren.

I discovered that Margaret was quite keen on looking at pictures but the numbers and letters made little sense.

However, each day, her vocabulary increased as far as speech was concerned and some of her memory of the house started to return with the familiar things of home surrounding her.

Now, visitors called at the house instead of going to the hospital, though there were still lots of anxious phone-callers who had just received their Christmas cards or heard by word-of-mouth.

Whenever I use the phrase 'word-of-mouth', it takes me back to my occasional lecturing days at South Glamorgan College of Further Education as it used to be known.

I was having a spot of bother with the ladies attending the post-lunch management course. They had a tendency to chatter and distracted everyone else from hanging on to my every word.

The topic on that day was 'Communication' – perhaps a bit dull, but what management topic isn't? The section under discussion was those sets of initials that look familiar but do not necessarily convey an accurate idea of their meaning. TLA's (short for 'Three-Letter Acronyms') are a prime example.

For instance, everyone has heard of BBC and ITV and immediately understands what the initials represent. When it comes to the hospital scene, the acronyms may be a bit more confusing. There are such things as ICU's and PBU's in hospitals to name but a couple.

In order to stop the whispered conversations about last night's TV or new shoes or whatever, I put up on the board the word 'WOMAN' in block capitals with each letter in order in a column on the left side of the board.

Next, I asked for ideas of what it might mean or what the letters stood for. No one came up with an answer, but all the chitchat stopped suddenly and an unnatural silence reigned supreme.

Ok, so I am not too proud of what happened next, but let us say that it was expedient and I never had any more problems with noise from the ladies attending the course.

I filled in the blanks next to the letters as follows. On the first line, I added the letters 'ORD'. On the second, I added an 'F', and on the third, 'OUTH'. Then on the fourth, 'D' and on the fifth, 'AUSEUM'.

Sorry, girls, but it was expedient at the time.

The males in the class shouted and laughed and applauded.

The ladies retained their earlier sudden silence, but I had made my point.

Not that I have anything against women – rather the reverse, I suspect. In my professional capacity, I did a lot to make improvements in working conditions for the female staff. On one occasion, I actually split a historically male full-time job into two part-time posts to make it suitable for either sex.

The male/female issue has raised its ugly head in my published work. In one of my scientific publications I once referred to 'Man', with a capital 'M', while writing about the species – as you do, if you are a scientist.

One lady in the profession deigned to write a letter of complaint to the magazine publishers about this. I responded to the publisher by insisting that I had used the normal terminology used in scientific terms as '*MAN, the species*'.

As a rider, I added that I was in no way anti-feminist and had watched with detached interest while women '*Burnt their Bra's*' in public and then looked around for support'.

Despite my *faux pas* with the unintentional pun, this was then published to my surprise. On the plus side, it had the effect of silencing any further comment from the feminine lobby.

But, I digress, as they say.

Back to business.

It was some time before I realised the significance of the Scout-stamped Christmas cards. They had been posted on the day of the accident and so, lacked the vital insert telling the tale of Margaret's accident. In fact two of our fairly close local friends did not find out for several weeks after the event, even though I personally told one of their close acquaintances on the day after the accident.

It is all about our failure to communicate effectively under stress (well, mine in this instance). Also, any gossip seems to have 'Heineken' qualities in contrast to important news. (Thus gossip will reach parts that other news misses as they infer in the advert).

On Monday morning, I had placed a request for someone from our GP Surgery to attend to check Margaret's blood pressure. I was religiously doling out her newly prescribed pills for controlling her blood pressure without any idea of the consequences.

In the hospital everything had been monitored regularly throughout the day. Sadly, there was no way for me to continue checking how well the pills were controlling Margaret's blood pressure. I saw it as important to maintain a reasonable level of blood pressure in order to prevent another bleed into her brain.

One of our friends had suffered a second stroke because her blood pressure was erratic and went sky-high. Here was a possible risk that I did not wish to take.

Our son heard me repeat the request to the GP Surgery on the following day and decided to do something about it himself. He went into town to do some Christmas shopping and came back with a blood pressure monitor. From then on, I checked Margaret's blood pressure twice a day – morning and evening – for the next three years.

The clinic nurse turned up *five days later* and checked Margaret's pressures. How useful is that? She got the same result as I had obtained, but by then, I was quite well versed in the practice.

Ten years on, because of the pills we both now take, we still record blood pressure and pulse each morning as a precaution. Each month, I plot the results and do averages on the computer. Then I plot yearly figures for the same at the end of each year. Well, isn't that why we have computers?

Doctors will tell you that such things are of little use to a patient. But these results proved vital later on in the forthcoming Millennium Year, as you will probably gather as time goes by.

There was no point in cancelling my request now that I had a blood-pressure monitor. The nurse's results gave me an opportunity to check our electronic instrument against the standard clinic monitor – something that was very important and very necessary apparently.

I need not have worried. The nurse's results had matched mine. Since that time, I have had our monitor checked frequently at the Surgery and it has always been spot on.

On 23rd December, just over a month after the accident, we made the journey along the M4 to Reading and spent Christmas and Boxing Day with our elder son and his family. Neil followed us down the M4 with his own agenda, since he planned to visit some of his old UK buddies while he had the chance.

One of the immediate benefits of the move was that I was able to relax a little. The grandchildren were superb, making sure that Grandma was comfortable and entertained. They showed Grandma how to play simple games, stretching her brain a little at the same time.

Because I was still recovering from the 'Flu, Neil did all the things I normally do such as lifting the twins to the ceiling upside down in order to allow them to walk along the ceiling. You know what it is like with two-and-a-half year-olds.

Despite their tender age, the grandchildren seemed to sense that Grandma was disorientated. It was during their exchanges that I first noticed Margaret's inability to pronounce the first letter of most words.

There was a hesitancy of speech. A stumbling over the words.

The children hardly noticed it because they were experiencing the same difficulty, especially with longer words with which they were unfamiliar. I consider that, because of this, they got along just fine.

These conversations gave me the idea that Margaret's brain was behaving rather like a child's in that it was discovering new words all the time and learning how to pronounce them as well as how to use them.

Okay, so I am nuts and what do I know about anything. Some brilliant psychologist or brain specialist is going to laugh their socks off at that preposterous idea.

According to my psychedelic dream of a couple of weeks ago, Margaret's word database in her head was missing the slots for the alphabetical storage of the first letter of the longer words. As far as I could work out, the hypothesis had a fair degree of sense in it. Even so, when she tried to retrieve a word, the message to the muscles of her mouth was out of sync, stopping her from saying the word correctly. I think the doctors call it 'aphasia'.

Later in the year 2000, we were to find the ideal people for Margaret to converse with – people who had to pause before replying, but for a very different reason. These were people who did not have aphasia, but were usually quite normal in their speech. They were French and German holiday-makers on a week-long river cruise. They all wanted to try out their 'English' on us.

Back to the present. On Christmas Eve, we took the twins to the Crib Service at the local Church and it was lovely to see how they interacted with all the other children. The children also knew some of the Christian Christmas characters – learned from their Nursery School.

They could sing some of the Christmas Carols and made a fuss of the baby in the crib. It all went down very well with Margaret as well as the children.

The twins had excitedly told us earlier that they had 'Seen the Man', (Santa Claus) in Reading when they had been out shopping with their mother earlier in the day.

On Christmas morning, the grandchildren were in awe of the fact that Santa Claus had been. They just looked at all the wrapped presents and made no attempt to unwrap them.

My granddaughter Pippa, poked about under the decorated Christmas tree and found a small gift that bore her name.

In the midst of all the larger boxes wrapped in Christmas paper, she said to her brother, Terry, '*Oh, look. This one has my name on it. If there is not one for you, then you can share mine*'.

Now that really did bring tears to my eyes.

Boxing Day was a quieter affair. The children were immersed in their new toys. Margaret was trying to get involved in what they were doing or watching and learning from their parents who were busily preparing the meals.

I found myself falling asleep at the drop of the proverbial Santa Claus hat. Our younger son was still out visiting some of his old friends from University days, or friends from old work-places up and down the country.

For me, the Christmas holiday period proved quieter and more restful than usual, though it was at times frenetic when it came to preparing the meals. I continued to recover from the 'flu, but kept a safe distance between myself and the family and no one caught my bug, I am pleased to say.

We were all due to de-camp elsewhere on December 27th. Our younger son Neil was off on his skiing trip to the French Alps.

Margaret and I left after lunch for our Bournemouth hotel and so there were some tearful goodbyes. The grandchildren and their parents would have their home back. The visit had helped Margaret quite a lot and some of the glaze had gone from her eyes. She was still pretty helpless though.

The story of how the Bournemouth trip came about is quite amazing. Early in November, three weeks before the accident, my wife had booked us into a hotel in Bournemouth for a 'tween' break (between Christmas and New Year).

We have done this for a couple of years now and find that it serves several purposes. It is usually quieter after all the festivities. We can ease ourselves away from the family without offence and we can go to the sales every day without worrying about meals and things.

I had packed a few warm clothes along with the essentials for Margaret. The selection of evening-wear was fairly minimal but it hardly mattered. It was not as if we were going to evening functions or parties.

The trip down to Bournemouth was wet if uneventful. The persistent light rain stopped as the lights of Bournemouth appeared and the town itself was quite dry when we arrived. Our room in the hotel was nice and cosy. The food was quite good for hotel food and there was always a good selection on the Menu.

We were on half-board – Breakfast and Evening Meal.

This allowed us to do all our usual Bournemouth activities. We would visit the Sales. Buy up bargain-priced Christmas card packs for next year plus wrapping paper and fancy string and trimmings. We planned to visit the coastal towns and walk along the cliff-top frontage.

Margaret quickly settled into the pattern and really seemed to enjoy the freedom and the joy of deciding what to do each day. Perhaps the familiar pattern of previous trips was getting through the mists of her brain.

For the past few years, the weather on the South Coast between Christmas and New Year had been dry and sunny with sharp frosts each morning. Our visit this time was no exception.

A quiet walk down through the gardens in the lovely sunshine - taking care on the frosty footpaths - was wonderfully invigorating. The shops were not exactly full that year and we were able to visit several of the big department stores advertising their post-Christmas Sales by taking a rest in a coffee shop between excursions.

We bought some sandwiches for lunch and wandered back to the hotel for a welcome cup of tea and a little sleep. Then it was out to the Sales again.

The weather had turned really icy on the second day so that we had to watch our step in the morning. The walk beside the Bourne stream down to the Winter Gardens was not easy. As a reward for our endeavour, we were able to enjoy some seaside ozone as we climbed up the hill for the stroll along the clifftops of Eastcliff beside the sea.

On the way back, we bought ourselves a sandwich from one of the Take-Away's and took it back to our room for lunch.

The sandwich was duly washed down with a cup of tea. Then afterwards, we took another little nap before going out again. It was beginning to become a habit.

Christchurch has always been a favourite haunt and so I got the car out and took Margaret over to wander that lovely town's shops and the riverside. The weather was a bit brisk to say the least, but it was good to be out in the fresh air.

When our eldest son was very young, we used to push him on the swings in the little children's park on the right of the main road, just as you come to the edge of town.

From Christchurch, I drove over to the bustling ferry-town of Lymington. There, we parked the car and walked the town, then sauntered down to see the ferry that goes across to the Isle of Wight.

There were several Cafés on the main street so we had another cup of tea to warm us up before returning to Bournemouth.

On the way down to Lymington, there were quite a few signs on white posts at the road junctions with fingers pointing to local places either side of the main road. As we had travelled along the road, I would point to a sign and tell Margaret what it said. I did this at each sign to try to interest her in her surroundings.

The road we took on our return journey was quite winding in places. Stuck in the hedge at one of the bends was an ancient piece of dog-eared chipboard about two foot wide and three foot high originally. The board was dirty, but brush-stroked across it in rather runny red paint was the two-word missive,

HORSE
MANURE

To my utter surprise and amazement, Margaret turned and pointed at the sign. *'Look'*, she said rather haltingly as I slowed to take the corner, *'Horse Manure'*.

The words were not too distinct but there was no doubt in my mind that those were the words she uttered.

Those two words were the first words that Margaret had been able to read since the accident. After that, if she asked me to read a sign that whizzed past the window and out of my sight on her side of the car, I would say, *'Horse Manure'*.

This would produce a peal of joyous laughter from her as she realised that I had not seen the sign.

Bournemouth had been a good idea. The booking had been made months before the accident.

It gave our family the chance to see Margaret ('Grandma') in the usual way for a few days over Christmas. Then it allowed us both a bit of molly-coddling at the hotel where we could relax and get to know each other again.

There were, unfortunately some events relating to Margaret's ongoing care that might have had a different outcome if I had let the Hospital discharge Margaret in the normal way.

This is a grey area in the order of things. So it is difficult for me to contemplate what benefits in the way of help might have transpired if I had not asked for Margaret to be released into my care. Maybe that is all 'pie-in-the-sky', or more likely, just a figment my imagination.

Chapter Four
Training and retraining

Apart from the normal home visit to see that we were coping, Dr Olds had written up some follow-up treatment such as speech therapy and occupational therapy for Margaret. The home visit never materialised and the occupational therapy never happened. The speech therapy did not start until March, 2000, some three months later.

I believe I mentioned my concerns in that direction in one of the earlier chapters on the subject of 'too many administrators, not enough professional staff'.

While Margaret would have benefited from some professional help in home-craft, there is no doubt in my mind that the speech therapy arrived at the right time for her. This you will probably be able to judge for yourself as her recovery state unfolds. It is only if things had not happened the way they did that the absence of the immediate speech therapy might have proved problematical.

Our ninety-minute sessions before breakfast with the children's books - doing word games and alphabetical games - continued to be an ongoing feature of each morning with Margaret – even when we were on holiday.

In one of the three books that I used, the alphabet was in block capitals fortunately, because of Margaret's inability to read the small letters of the alphabet at that stage in her recovery. It was broken up into sections of five consecutive letters denoted by five colours in sequence.

We would go through the green letters, the blue ones, and the yellow ones etc so that Margaret got used to recognising the shape of the letters in whatever order I chose. It took about three months for her to master the alphabet. I had very little success with the numbers though.

I also devised some 'flash' cards in black ink with both upper and lower case letters. There were certain of the small letters that Margaret experienced a high degree of difficulty in understanding. Coincidentally, these were the same letters that started the words that she always stumbled on when she tried to say something. The letters were b, d, m, n, p, q, u, w, y and possible h.

d	b	u	w	y
q	p	n	m	h

You may see some similarity between these letters in that 'b' and 'd' are mirror images as are 'p' and 'q'. But then 'p' is 'b' upside down as is 'q' an upside down 'd'.

There are the same similarities between 'n' and 'u' and 'm' and 'w'. Further, 'y' itself is really 'u' with a tail as is 'h' an 'n' with a tail.

('w' might be considered as double 'u' or 'uu').

During the ninety or so minutes of each morning session, we spent time on some of those awful photocopy pictures that Margaret had been tested on during her therapy at the West Wing hospital.

Over time, I as able to unearth some more acceptable line drawings from which Margaret could identify objects. We also looked at the illustrated children's dictionary so that Margaret could relate pictures to words eventually.

Sometimes, her conversational ability amazed me. In conversation, Margaret could often say words with which she had previously experienced extreme difficulty. This would manifest itself either in our speech-training or comprehension sessions, or when using the 'Children's First Dictionary' only a few minutes earlier.

I could never understand whether this was normal recall from another piece of brain or if the brain had taken in the information from our efforts with the book.

I favoured the former idea because we tend to build sentences and associate words as a normal part of conversation. In other words, our conversation and writing tends to be stereotyped, or reflex in origin. It is that feature which gives us our own individual identity in speech and text composition.

Did I just write that?

Wow!

What it means is that, if we listen to someone speaking on the radio, or pick up the phone, we can instantly identify the person speaking because of their individual voice characteristics.

Each day, rain or shine, we continued with our browsing of the 'Children's First Dictionary'. Some days would be good and we would cover up to five different initial letters with sample words. Other days it would be only two or three different letters before my wife got tired.

Still, Margaret found little difficulty with uppercase (capital) letters. Yet several of the lowercase (small) letters continued to give her problems. I can understand Cyrillic writing and spotted that she liked to say 'V' for 'B' or vice-versa. But again, the significance of any of it really escaped me.

Once, on a day of deep depression, Margaret said that she could not manage to do any of the words or letters. I did not ever make the mistake of insisting on her doing anything if she decided not to try. In this way, she built up confidence in my judgment.

If I ever spotted that she was tiring, I would stop immediately, even though I wanted her to do more and to succeed. Training had to be fun, not a tiring chore!

Margaret's progress from awkwardly transcribing her name in capitals during the second week of her hospitalisation to actually making simple diary entries by week four was a remarkable achievement in my book and says much for her courage and determination.

I was a bit concerned about my computer courses and customers. The business was fast disappearing and there was no time to research new contracts and customers to keep it all going. Besides, the word was out concerning my predicament and so, valued customers went elsewhere.

Chapter Five
Recriminations

As time passed and Margaret improved, I became even more determined that my wife would get back as much of her previous life as it was possible to do. Her progress in just a few short weeks was amazing and this helped to spur me on to recover Margaret's ability in other key areas of her life.

The total lack of support services from the established institutions of health and social services proved to be a severe stumbling block to progress, as did the attitude of any of the government organisations we contacted for help from time to time. We seemed to have disappeared off the map as far as support was concerned.

I penned a little ditty - which I have produced below to describe our situation.

From the time she left hospital on December 18 1999 to January 18 2000, Margaret received only two visits from the District Nurse (that I managed to get going after a mere three phone calls to the Surgery on each occasion).

I also arranged for her to see her GP, Dr Gethin Welland. (This latter was as ever, prompted by a phone call from me rather than any prescribed follow-up health care).

On Strokes

It is certainly no joke
When your spouse has a stroke
And Social Services fail to support you.
So you give up your life
To look after your wife,
Hoping God is still there to protect you.

John Greenridge, 2009.

The lack of post-discharge care was evidenced by its complete absence. This in direct contrast to the assurances from Dr Olds, her Consultant in the Stroke Unit that there would be regular check-ups by the District Nurse, plus physiotherapy and speech therapy. This post-hospital care should have included keeping a wary eye on her blood pressure as well as daily support from the therapists.

Margaret was promised two home visits per week from the Speech Therapist. This latter was a joke. Before you qualify for home visits, you require assessment of the need.

When I enquired, the University Hospital Outpatient's Clinic contacted us to say that there was an eight-week waiting list for assessment in the Speech Therapy Department! They had not the specialist staff to cope. What this meant in real terms was that we were very much on our own and left to our own devices.

Was it ever so?

Right from the start, one of the subjects that kept coming onto the agenda in surreptitious ways during conversations with our friends about the cause of the accident was the question of retribution. This pressure to do something gave me serious problems because it interfered with the main priority of nursing Margaret back to health. I had too much to do without getting involved in litigation as well. I needed time to think about that side of things.

From quite early on, I did take some daily diary notes as a guide to what had taken place and when it had all happened. Then I took some photographs of the paving blocks in Church Street. I also sought advice from a Solicitor.

First of all, I rang up the ARP50 legal hotline. The legal advisor gave me the telephone number of the Law Society, who were extremely helpful in providing guidance and possible outcomes of strategies and agreed to put me in touch with an accident specialist in my area.

This all sounds exciting and positive but alas, it came to naught because the suggested Solicitor had moved on a couple of years previously, or so I was informed.

A new unknown Solicitor from the same firm - whom the Law Society had not recommended, let it be said - wanted to come to the house to interview Margaret. My dearly beloved was still languishing in hospital at the time, struggling to get to grips with making a cup of tea all by herself in the kitchen annex across the corridor from her room in the Stroke Unit, so that was a no-no.

A couple of weeks later, an ex-colleague of Margaret and a dear friend, suggested the 0800 number advertised on ITV and this was what I eventually used. With one enquiring phone call, their organisation swung into action and we were put on course for an interview with one of their assessors.

Another thing that had bothered me all those weeks was that I had not had time to report the accident to the Council Authorities. I was most concerned about this omission now that I was aware of the number of accidents that happened on an almost daily basis in Church Street, Cardiff. I rang up the Highways number in the local directory and was given the correct number to phone.

In my personal opinion, the accident had most likely happened because of faulty maintenance to the paved area. This may have been coupled to a perhaps, too cavalier approach by Cardiff City Council to the idea of re-laying the base to the existing paving in Church Street. In view of the proposed renewal of the paving to be installed at a later date, this was hardly surprising.

The reason for allowing the now loose slabs to be taken up for whatever purpose in the first place was not in dispute. The checking of any re-laying was most definitely the Council's responsibility. The street paving had been allowed to get into a poor state of repair. This was exacerbated by the fact that heavy delivery lorries including a brewer's dray, regularly used the route for access.

The Planning Office and Building Regulations Office probably provided sanction for any work on the adjacent buildings initially. This would include provision for digging up the street to access mains gas, water and electricity at least, if not drainage and the subsequent repair.

There are unquestionably appropriate operating procedures and safety standards and inspections of the work in order to avoid destruction of the paving and to maintain the highway. These guys are usually meticulous about such checks. Church Street was a busy pedestrian area in the heart of the city. But it had lost its way.

The Highway Authority should be able to provide any maintenance and inspection schedules. There must be plenty of information to support a case against the Council. I decided to do some investigating myself and jotted down some likely sources of information.

In those days, many of the slabs in Church Street lay at an angle to the horizontal and some were cracked or had huge gaps separating the slabs. Several slabs moved when stepped on like something out of an Indiana Jones film. One slab was not only cracked and loose, but large sections of the slab were actually missing, leaving a two-three inch (60mm) drop to the base sand layer of the pavement at that point.

According to some of the local traders I surveyed, accidents happened every day in Church Street.

While I was taking photographs to illustrate the then current state of the paving, my wife and I were continually interrupted in our work by people stopping to say that they had fallen in Church Street. One man said that his wife fractured her leg and now had four steel pins holding it together. Another man said that he had broken his wrist.

(Note: Since I wrote this, the whole area has been taken up and some excellent granite sets laid along the full length of the street).

I contacted the Police CCTV Unit to find out if they had a tape of the incident, but so far I have heard nothing, which looks like a negative. There are CCTV cameras all over Cardiff but they are not much use when they do not record an incident and that proved to be the case!

The Chief Engineer for roads and highways should be in a position to provide details of the incidence of reported accidents. He may also be able to provide information about the problems in Church Street when it rains. He might also know what happens to sand when it gets wet (it liquefies) and what effect this has on the slabs when heavy vehicles traverse the affected area under those conditions.

I was aware that both the mud from under the sand layer and the sand itself were clearly visible around the edges of each paving stone. These elements had been forced up through the natural gaps at the edges of each paving slab as water had seeped into the base layer, causing liquefaction of the sand and mud.

So there should be plenty of sources of information if I needed them to support a Case.

But in the end, it was all unnecessary hyperbole. No one investigated anything – not even the staining of my wife's clothes, or the evidence provided by her shoes. So much for American TV's legal soaps like 'Quincy' or 'Ironside' where they prove everything using sophisticated forensic evidence. Nothing like that happened in our case.

One day while visiting the Bank and doing some town shopping, I tripped over a new but cracked paving block in The Hayes, Cardiff, which is around the corner from Church Street. The Hayes was covered with the same surface paving as Church Street at the time.

An area outside Waterstones bookshop had been recently re-laid with temporary matching blocks ahead of a brand new scheme for repaving the whole area. I noticed that most of the newly laid slabs were cracked. I presumed that this was due to a faulty underlay, if that is the correct term. Alternatively, it may well have been due to excessive force being used to try to level off the blocks.

Until the new initiative for an extended pedestrianised area came on stream, I anticipated more problems for pedestrians due to this temporary and faulty repair of the paved surface. Why was this allowed to happen in the face of the strict regulations regarding maintenance of street paving? Surely there are rules and inspections for such repair work!

Chapter Six
Towards Normality

I have never before experienced such a stir in any church as when my wife entered our Church on Sunday 9th January 2000. It was like a Royal Wedding when the bride appears. Amazingly, the congregation stood as she entered and applauded her all the way to her usual seat.

The following Sunday, 16 January (Margaret's birthday) the Minister of our Church, Mr. Churchman, expressed to the congregation his joy at seeing Margaret in Church again. He also mentioned his disappointment at being absent the previous Sunday, thus missing the standing ovation given to Margaret by the congregation on her first visit to Church since the accident occurred.

Next day, Monday 17 January was the day the lady from the Stroke Association arranged to call on us in an effort to help us sort out some of our problems. A few pointers were all we were looking for.

She was due to come in the evening at 7pm. Margaret was a bit concerned because some of her work colleagues had rung up to say that they would be coming on the same evening at 7.30pm. I told her not to worry since the second lot would terminate the first meeting and stop it going on longer than I assumed to be necessary.

In the event, the Stroke Association lady phoned from her home in Penarth – just along the coast from Cardiff - to say that it was too foggy to come and made an appointment for daytime on the Monday following. This fog did not prevent the ladies from work coming later in the evening since there was little or no fog inland, or up in the Welsh Valleys to worry about.

These lovely friends and ex-workmates duly arrived with another basket of fruit and provided news and gossip enough to make the evening bright and interesting. I think the ladies were amazed at the improvement in Margaret because they were expecting someone really ill, or bed-ridden, or severely handicapped. The conversational glitches were few and far between and I was delighted with the evening.

On Tuesday evening, Margaret was collected from home by two of her friends from the Flower Club and escorted down to the local Memorial Hall for the dem'. Her reception was similar to the first appearance in church. She created quite a stir. Everyone wanted to say, '*Hello, welcome back*', and congratulate her on her recovery.

Prior to her arrival a couple of her floral colleagues had been arguing because one said that she had seen and spoken to Margaret when she was out shopping. The other person - who had visited Margaret in hospital and knew all about her brain injury - said that it was not possible for her to be out of hospital yet, let alone out shopping. I guess Margaret's arrival settled that argument.

I hope you appreciate the value as much as we do of having such staunch, reliable friends in dire situations.

After lunch next day, the man from a firm called 'Claims Direct' came to the house to discuss a possible claim in relation to the accident. He was a pleasant guy who knew what he was about.

Naturally, he asked lots of questions and filled in lots of different forms. He told anecdotes of claims that were ongoing and some that had failed for obvious reasons. We kept him inadequately supplied with tea and all the information needed for the forms he had to complete.

The 'Claims Direct' man wanted as much information as possible and took a copy of my notes and some of my photographs of the area where the accident occurred. These latter I had conveniently taken in advance of his visit. (Here's some I prepared earlier!). It would take some time for the firm of Solicitors he represented to say whether they were willing to take the case or not.

One thing he told me to do was to keep a daily diary. Another was to keep all Bills for extra help or anything to do with the accident including phone calls and letters. Unfortunately, the Law moved the goalposts to our disadvantage before our claim was settled, so I think we lost out a bit in the end. Was it ever so?

The next day, our very close friend Ellen Rowe arrived mid-morning to show Margaret how to make marmalade from Seville oranges. Now I ought to tell you that Margaret has made marmalade almost every year without even consulting a cook-book.

Needless to say, I was left instructions for boiling and simmering for the next morning's follow-up lesson. I am now an expert simmerer, but the philosophy of the cooking procedure still escapes me. I think I'll stick to what I already know - boiling kettles to make tea, make my coffee in the microwave, the occasional fine omelette and smooth custard.

We rose early on Thursday to start off the marmalade. All the bits had been prepared on the previous day and it was just a question of putting it all together and cooking.

While I was simmering the marmalade stock, (Ho, Ho!), Margaret was busy. She was laboriously copying some previously discussed and agreed text onto 'Thank You' cards to thank all the people for their good wishes and tangible support.

This was a task that she seemed determined to conquer. But from my point of view it was an important learning exercise for her in both reading and writing. I recall doing similar exercises when I was in Junior School. They were called 'lines' and were given for some misdemeanor.

There was also a small element of comprehension because Margaret would keep bringing the text to me for reassurance and interpretation of the meaning of words and phrases.

These enquiries occurred whatever I was doing and wherever I was at the time. I was standing naked in the bathroom cleaning my teeth and I foolishly took the electric toothbrush out of my mouth to say the phrase she was unsure about.

White drops of saliva-diluted toothpaste went everywhere - but I discovered that it gives a nice polish on the bathroom tiles when wiped off with a towel! We both laughed when it happened and I felt that it was so important to keep smiling and see the funny side of these minor incidents.

At this time, since none of the expected support from the NHS or Social Services mentioned by Margaret's Consultant had materialized. I felt very much alone in the battle to improve my wife's health and to retrain her memory from scratch.

To help with the basic domestic work, I decided to hire someone from a home-care service to come in once a week. This should give me a couple of hours of Carer relief. I made a few phone calls after consulting Yellow Pages and the Local Thomson's Directory.

At last, on Friday 21 January - over a month since leaving hospital, some outside help arrived. It was private help of course. Neither Health Service, nor County Council care and support services for the elderly and infirm.

I had a job to get it even paying for it. The first organisation I contacted sent an under-stamped brochure that cost me £0.34 extra postage to receive. It was no good to me and I should have just sang, *'Return to sender'*, to the postman. ('Sang' in that sense is a euphemism, since my voice is barely musical).

I wanted some morning tuition for my wife so that she could re-learn some skills. 'Welsh Care' could only provide afternoon help. (Margaret was better in the mornings before she had a chance to tire).

The same was true for the next private organisation we tried – 'Community Care' - but I managed to buy some help between 11am and 1pm. This, we tried for two weeks.

The first lady who arrived was quick and efficient. She was pleasant and dressed in a white coat for working in.

I explained to her that we did not really need a cleaner *per se* and she agreed that the house was immaculate. She helped my wife with changing two duvets to winter-weight from summer-weight. This is a difficult job for one under any circumstance and proved to be a worthwhile exercise for Margaret.

The main work needed that day was to spring-clean the food cupboard and replace the paper liners to the shelves. Margaret was delighted with what the two of them working in tandem accomplished but, on the minus side, she was too tired to eat lunch and had to go to bed for a while.

Unfortunately for us, this nice, welcome lady was filling in for someone else. When the assigned person took over, the second lady did not do any of the tasks I asked of her. She broke things and only cleaned to the level we normally started at.

There are cleaners and there are also those that I refer to as 'muck-spreaders'. I suppose our scientific backgrounds account for our higher standard of expectation. After that first session, Margaret was so tired that I tried to change the work schedule to two one-hour sessions but could not do so. The system couldn't cope with that.

These 'Carers', as they were referred to, were good at conversation and making cups of tea but little else was satisfactory. I put up with it for a few weeks because of the company it provided for Margaret, but eventually stopped it in favour of a gardener.

The gardener we hired was called Sandy. She was a mature lady with a grown up family.

Sandy was studying garden design at College and was looking for some practical work to help her College studies. Our garden was ideal for this purpose since it contained some specimen plants and a huge variety of verbiage that needed attention at intervals throughout the year.

Sandy worked hard and was a welcome change from the home-care service. More importantly, having a gardener allowed Margaret the additional pleasure of getting back into the marvellous garden she adored, so it was doubly satisfying.

Margaret suddenly looked forward to Sandy's weekly visits. The garden - neglected for three months - started to look more normal and things were being done in season.

Some ten years on, we still employ the same gardener. She is now virtually a family friend. Her health has not been all that good of late though and Margaret will really miss her company if she has to give up as a gardener.

One of the highlights of our life was the weekly shopping trip. I made a list of things we needed (which usually missed off something vital and important). Margaret had the job of paying for the goods in order to teach her about money.

She could manage all right on her own when she had time to prepare at the till. However, if I let her help with packing the food into plastic bags, she would get flustered at the till and then say, *'I can't manage this today'.*

By the eighth week (end of January), Margaret was using phrases such as 'thring dings' to mean 'three rings on the telephone'. Three rings was our in-house signal to mean, 'I'm on my way' or 'Come and collect me from a pre-arranged spot'.

Our conversations were often hilariously funny as she struggled with pronunciation, or to find the correct word for a sentence of speech. There were plenty of occasions when she would halt in mid-sentence - or even mid-word - and say, *'No, I've lost it'* or *'I've forgotten'.*

We always laughed about it in a friendly way and I would tell her to forget it. The brain had obviously hit an impasse, or run out of steam.

'It will sort itself out in a few minutes', I suggested and that was that for the moment.

That day gave us two new words to add to our ever-growing list of oddities. 'Snoochies and Koochies'.

My wife got up early - about 6am for the loo. It was a cold morning and a bit early for a cuppa, so she went back to bed for a quick snooze and to get cosy again.

She described the event to me an hour later when I rose at my usual time and brought her a cup of tea, the words snooze and cosy came out as Snoochies and Koochies - a far more interesting approach to the mundane, since I had no idea what Koochies were for quite a while.

For our evening meal, I chopped up potatoes, carrots, swede and celery. Meanwhile Margaret chopped and fried some onions and some garlic as our friends had recently taught her. She made a white sauce with cornflour, I think, while I prepared some broccoli and cabbage.

We were having a vegetable pie crusted with cornflakes and cheese.

We cooked everything but the greens. Those I did in the pressure-cooker. The sauce and the veg were mixed together and topped with the cheese and cornflakes and then grilled.

I reckon that I could possibly repeat that exercise at a pinch if I ever needed to do it for myself. But then again, perhaps that was all 'pie in the sky' as far as my own limited cooking brain was concerned.

Yesterday, I forgot to tell you that Margaret wrote some more 'Thank You' notes (on folded cards I had designed on the computer).

The cards displayed a nice 'Thank You' message on the inside page and Margaret printed/scrawled in her best effort at writing on the facing page where she thanked people for special things like visits to hospital, flowers etc.

She completed a further three cards before breakfast and was starting to join-up some of the letters as her speed and accuracy improve. Her reading skills were very good that day. She needed very little prompting from me on some quite difficult words.

I had a customer to visit and shopping to do. When I arrived back home, Margaret was busy hoovering the hallway. I hoped she had rested between activities since she tired easily - a typical phenomenon of stroke and head-injury patients apparently.

Whenever she felt tired, she would retire to bed to lie down for a while and quite often dropped off to sleep. This was in direct contrast to her previously busy lifestyle.

In her pre-accident life, it was unusual to find her in bed or resting before nine or ten o'clock in the evening. She had always been - as her workmates referred to her - 'the fastest thing on two legs' in my book.

'We will be making some more quiche today', (it says in my diary).

I say 'we' because that's how it goes at the moment. I carefully break the eggs into a saucer and add them separately into the bowl with the milk. Four lovely quiche - two with bacon and two with mushrooms.

This was exciting stuff on the edge of actual cookery for me. I usually had to peel potatoes and scrape carrots but this was the real thing, or as close as I was ever likely to get. Pastry was quite beyond me.

Wednesday turned out to be a day of mini-disasters. Our first real test of faith in and hope for, the future. The day started with pea soup of the freezing fog variety and it was my day for going to Cowbridge.

It was also the day the yellow 'Free-Ads' paper came out with the advert for selling Margaret's VW Polo car. There seemed little point in hanging on to her car since the steering would be too tough for her to manage with safety if she ever got back to driving.

We had discussed buying her a car with power steering and I had gone ahead with the VW Polo advertisement on the strength of that conversation. Not that we had even imagined that she would be driving for some time to come at that stage of her recovery.

The phone started ringing shortly after nine am. - something I had not anticipated. I had left home at eight knowing that someone would collect my wife and take her to a 'Stroke Association' meeting that was due to start around ten.

The fog delayed everything and so the visit did not go as well as expected. Still, she enjoyed herself to a point. I had arranged to pick up Margaret before twelve on my way back from Cowbridge - a convenient-enough idea.

I duly arrived back at the Centre where the Stroke Association meeting was held at just after eleven-thirty and so I elected to wait until the meeting finished.

Unfortunately, due to the earlier delay due to the fog, this was not until nearly an hour later. I sipped the rest of my coffee from the flask (another one I had prepared earlier, as they say) and listed to Radio I, II and IV as well as the two commercial channels. Fortunately, the car was warm from the journey, but I really regretted the waste of time. There was little enough of it around at the moment.

By the time we arrived home I was aware of impending disaster. Margaret told me that she had fielded about eight to ten calls from prospective buyers before being picked up and taken to the meeting. She had handled the situation most admirably by taking down names and telephone numbers including time of call and a few other incidentals. Each was on a separate 'numbered' piece of old Christmas Card.

Her ability to organise such information amazed me. The numbers were all over the place and some were incomplete or unrecognizable. She had tried really hard though and most of the names were there in crazily arranged block capitals. Margaret had not really mastered lower case letters yet.

There were more calls throughout the day. These would not have been a problem except that we were expecting some of our friends to call at the house at any minute. This deterred me from making any plans for people to view the car or arrive at decisions about the car's future. It was all happening too fast for comfort.

You may well wonder what decisions there were to make when the situation merely called for a 'Yes', or 'No', decision about selling the car to A or B. However, by this time Margaret was distraught about the thought of giving up the car she now regarded as the one on which she might relearn to drive again.

With such a philosophy, I began to wonder how our two boys had ever managed to cut the apron strings.

We asked our informal audience when they arrived. But they just talked around the problem, tending to agree with what either of us said.

Phone a friend?

We phoned our friend, Ellen Rowe about, of all things the price. It appeared that we were underselling the car by about £1000 possibly. Certainly another £500 was on the cards as a certainty.

I was appalled.

This accounted for the large number of calls. Anyone buying the car was on for an easy £500 and a dealer could go for the kill.

I took the only way out. Because of Margaret's increasing uncertainty and obvious unhappiness and concern, I withdrew the car from the market on compassionate grounds even though it grieved me to do so.

I would gladly have got rid of it so that I could have something easier for my dearly beloved to drive if she was able to take up driving again. Now, I would have to think again. It is not always easy to sell cars privately and to have a captive audience was a welcome change.

But the day was not finished.

The Social Worker from the Stroke Unit called to see how we were progressing.

I was able to offload some of my concerns in her direction. Apparently we should have received a visit from an Occupational Therapist at least to check that my wife was able to manage at home. It is called a 'home visit'. But we knew that already and it had made no difference to the obvious lack of support. This was always standard practice for stroke patients, but patently did not happen in our case, even though it was in Margaret's medical notes.

My impression had been that we would receive home visits for speech therapy as well. I must have forgotten that it was the National Health Service for a moment. In any case, the time for these visits had passed, though any sort of visit would have been a great help in the early stages of my wife's rehabilitation.

It was as if we had disappeared into a black hole and the NHS had conveniently forgotten that we existed. Carers may often be given help by the State in the form of 'Benefit' to pay for any services needed but no advice on that front was ever forthcoming.

And when I did get round to contacting the Benefit people, I wished that I had not spent all that time filling in their huge questionnaire – all in vain as you might already have guessed. Like all the other Social Services, they just didn't want to know.

How about some 'Disability Living Allowance' then?

I paid NHS, Employment Tax and Income Tax on my salary for nearly forty years. My wife did the same for nearly thirty years. We should have received some Benefit from all that. Then there were the Council Tax (previously 'Rates') payments for some 38 years, just to be going on with. We were both now on pensions, but none of this made any difference, apparently. We were very much left to our own devices.

The calls about the car continued well into my evening leisure, provoking an air of contriteness from Margaret. This I countered with euphoric anecdotes about her newfound ability to organise things and to take the lead in discussion.

If life is all doom and gloom, look for the silver lining. OK, so every silver lining has a huge cloud, but we must be positive in such dilemmas at least and determine which aspects are of importance and which of little or no consequence.

Tomorrow is another day.

Next day, after making a few calls, I pulled the plug on the phone again, unable to face paying the penalty for putting in the advert.

Our home economics friend Ellen Rowe arrived to show Margaret how to make a cake. Margaret invited her to stay on for lunch and, since the two women get on well, the day was a success. I would benefit from the lovely cakes in due course. Since my day went well after the bother of the last two days, we both felt good.

The Orange Badge I had applied for on Margaret's behalf via Dr Welland, her GP, arrived in the post, as did my new Internet Bible and our new M & S plastic cards.

I didn't even get around to having the latter verified on the previous occasion M & S sent me a shopping card. Is this due to the M & S marketing problem? Was I personally responsible for their economic slide? I suppose not, yet if all the husbands in the country shopped as I did last year, then the answer would be an emphatic 'YES'.

That evening we were all going to the Memorial Hall to see *'Allo 'Allo*. (Our local Amateur Theatrical Society does a play every now and again and these are all unmissable events).

As anticipated, it was bawdy, funny and enjoyable. Margaret laughed all the way through and an appreciative audience gave the cast plenty of support all night. I was inspired to shout, 'Encore' after one of Edith's famous songs, and even that got its laugh.

Friday dawned with another fit of depression from Margaret and poor performance on the reading score. Perhaps it was the effect of all that adrenaline running on the previous evening, or it might have been due to the return of the dreaded constipation.

The 'domestic' was due to arrive at eleven and so I hurried to think up a suitable work schedule for the two-hour spell. I remembered to put the words, 'Quality rather than quantity', against the work-plan before leaving for my computer class.

It was Mary's Birthday - an old friend from way back. This meant a slight detour on my way to Contract work through two sets of unwelcome roadworks.

As it turned out, despite my misgivings, the journey to Mary's house was too easy and as is usually the case, inevitably there was no reply when I got there.

Mary was out shopping.

I called in on the return journey and missed her again. A further call in the late afternoon elicited the same result. I left her birthday card with a little note.

The prezzy was just an eighth too big for the letter slot!

The potted chrysanths would maybe have squeezed in if I had stepped on them to flatten them. I'm sure that the process would not have produced 'pressed' flowers so I still had those to deliver as well as the prezzy.

Margaret had lost most of her depression when I got back at lunchtime. The domestic turned out to be one of the supervisors. Everything had gone well but as a parting gift, the lady broke the stand for our big ceramic roasting plate, that stands up on the corner shelf above the cook-books in the kitchen.

Margaret reminded me that the stand was a present from Mary.

The tragedy was that our helper was not due to put the plate back. She should not have touched the stand at all. It was not one of the prescribed tasks!

Later in the day, we were given a bit of a dilemma to sort out.

Prior to the accident, we would team up with two other families for a 'combined dinner party'. Each family would provide one course for the dinner. The host always provided main course and wine.

Our 'combined dinner' friends wanted us to stay with them for the weekend to give us both a well-earned rest from looking after ourselves. Our dear friend Ellen Rowe was also invited.

While the concept and the thought were well-founded, Margaret did not want to be away from home at the moment. She was trying hard to recover her identity and her sense of belonging. Her feelings about going out told her that 'home is best'.

Our grandchildren and their parents would like us to stay with them shortly. They have given us an open invitation just to come. That is another bridge we will have to cross. I think Margaret feels 'safe' in her own home for the present.

Neither Ellen Rowe - who was up to her eyes in family, lounge-floor wood blocks and itinerant workmen - or Margaret, were at all keen to be away from home at the moment.

I did not wish to be involved, since I had enough on my plate to sort out and preferred to follow the line of least resistance (Do I hear you say, 'Men - bloody useless in a crisis'?). Well, I think I can safely say that the last two months dispel any notions of cowardice in the face of enemy fire. LMF (Lack of Moral Fibre) just doesn't apply in my case.

The weekend passed almost unnoticed as we shopped, prepared meals and watched the box. Margaret was right. Home was best.

A letter arrived from the County Council enquiring about our Social Care needs and had we received their literature illustrating the services they offer.

Where were they a month ago when we were desperately seeking help and advice, I wonder? On their Christmas break I expect, or had the flu' like the rest of us. Probably someone mentioned our Orange Badge application and they responded to that. There must be some reason for the letter.

How wrong can you get?

When I found the time to have a good look at it, the letter turned out to be a 'Survey of Services' as supplied to the needy by the City Council.

They were not offering anything at all! They just wanted to know what services we were getting! I had misread the intention.

I placed an 'X' in all the 'No' boxes and sent it back in the stamped and addressed envelope. Some administrator would be happy that we were not creaming off his precious budget allowance. I wondered how much that administrative exercise cost the Cardiff ratepayers?

We did our weekly phone calls to friends and family on Sunday morning to relieve pressure on Sunday evening. Later, I took the opportunity to bottle a couple of gallons of wine that had been waiting for some time.

Once that job was out of the way, we tried out the electric organ, which had not been played for about two years, and Margaret tinkled a few piano keys. What a lovely day.

After an early dinner we were able to get cleared up before going out to the evening service at Church. This allowed us to take it gently after Church. We slipped away after seeing a few friends instead of going into the Hall for an après-Church cuppa.

Margaret was tired when we got home and asked me to put on her 'talking book' tape that our eldest had thoughtfully given as a Christmas gift. It was Elizabeth George's *'In pursuit of the proper sinner'*. I came up half-an-hour later to find her propped up in bed asleep. So much for talking books!

The following day I had to re-install the Internet on someone's computer. I discovered that the modem switched off its Internet connection if anyone made a telephone call on the handset. This was why the installation procedure had failed, I expect.

Anyway, I fixed it and for reward I was given another customer. And I'm talking of giving up the business? This stuff is mostly easy-peasy but there is one computer in Cardiff that failed to succumb to my charm, so I am not exactly infallible - yet!

The 'volunteer helper' from the Stroke Association came today and she was a charming ex-civil servant. Just what we needed. A bit like a meringue - all stiff and starch but nice when you get to know her.

Hilary, as she was called, solved my immediate dilemma.

The appointment with the Speech Therapist's assessment was at three on Thursday and lasted one hour. I had a computer class from one till three and since it was contract work, it was rather difficult to change. Our new volunteer offered to fill the gap and we gratefully accepted. So, another problem solved.

Hilary had developed an amateur interest in speech therapy and asked if she could sit in on the assessment to help her understand the process. I said that it was OK by us after Margaret agreed, though she should check that the Speech Therapy Department had no objections.

My reason for agreeing was dual fold. Margaret would have someone to sit with her throughout the session until I arrived about halfway through, I hoped. Our new helper would also get something out of it, which might make life easier for her charges as much as stimulating her interest.

Just occasionally, I found myself giving an involuntary sigh - about once a week or so. It always caught me unawares. I had one this morning in the middle of breakfast when I was thinking of nothing in particular.

Is this my brain telling me something I don't know or is it relief that all is well? In any case, I always felt slightly sad after the event as if something special had gone out of me forever.

Life was quite full and jolly at the moment, if that is the word. There was little to complain about except lack of rehabilitation help for my wife.

Even this took a small hesitant step towards resolution after yesterday's meeting with the volunteer from the Stroke Association.

The future looked bright and orange-badge now, yet I felt sad and unloved. It was unlike me to feel down. We all feel like that from time to time, I understand, so I hoped it would soon go. I felt as if I was missing something and I think I know what it was but that subject is not up for discussion, so let us press on regardless.

The visit to the Speech Therapy Department next day for the assessment proved to be physically demanding for Margaret. A whole hour of going through paper exercises choosing words, or objects from poor black and white photocopies of drawings and pictures. I was determined to do something about those poor photocopies when I had a bit of time.

I called a halt after the first half-hour had passed to allow Margaret to rest.

The Speech Therapist realized the problem and changed the strategy to include me in a discussion about progress and how I felt. I highlighted the problem about Margaret's conversation hitting a brick wall, metaphorically and was told that there were ways of overcoming this difficulty.

I kept silent about my feelings on the eight-week time-gap between leaving hospital and getting some help with her aphasia. Though I did manage to squeeze in a remark to the effect that we had been promised twice-weekly visits following discharge from hospital. This fell on deaf ears - which did not surprise me.

The girl doing all the work was a trainee with a strong regional Midlands accent. Not the ideal for teaching Margaret vowel pronunciation in my book. The actual therapist sat to one side and contributed very little. Her job was to see how the trainee went about the job of assessment. I would have preferred to have had Margaret assessed by the expert, if you see what I mean!

'C'est la vie', as they say.

Next day - Friday morning - dawned with Margaret feeling distinctly unwell and a little dizzy. Her blood pressure was down to 110/66 and I called the GP Surgery for the District Nurse to come to check it.

I would have run my wife round to the Surgery but I had another Contract to fulfill. Also, the Care-person was due later in the morning.

The receptionist on the telephone took down the details. He said that if I had not heard by lunchtime to ring again and he would get me fitted in for a 4.30 appointment at the Surgery.

All this was totally useless to me. The potential crisis was now.

I repeated the blood pressure and it was virtually identical.

I had noticed that Margaret's blood pressure was down a bit two days ago but had assumed that this was due to inactivity and her blood pressure pills. Of course as you might have guessed, when I phoned at twelve, nobody had been from the surgery to check. Margaret was feeling a bit better by that time.

When I got home, I redid the blood pressure and it had risen to 132/72, which was closer to the figures I had expected for her during a resting state.

Why am I the one making the decisions? I am not a doctor.

Where is the NHS? Where is the promised support?

Why can't I get it to respond when I need it?

After all, I have carried the can for nearly two months on a mere two nurse visits before Christmas and one visit to the Surgery after Christmas.

Where were all the back-up services I was promised?

Was I complaining yet again?

Margaret did not want me to make a fuss. So that was that.

❦

Time passed.

On February 8, 2000, we attended Geraint Olds' Outpatient Clinic.

It was now some seven weeks since my wife came out of hospital. The day of the first post-discharge appointment with the Consultant had arrived. We had to be at the Royal Infirmary Outpatient's Clinic for 11.15am.

As we went in the door, I recognised the place as the clinic I had attended when I broke my shoulder a few years back. The Infirmary was still active in those days and now, there was a distinct lack of buzz about the place.

The 'SEN' nurse advised me that our clinic was running to time and we would not have to wait for our allotted space. In the event, she was totally wrong and, some twenty-five minutes late, we were called - not to see the Consultant as we had imagined, but to see a new-to-us Houseman acting as a stand-in, I expect.

For starters, I showed him my computer-charts of Margaret's blood pressures and pulse over the period. Of course, the first thing he did was to check her BP and pulse.

The results were as I had expected.

We discussed the dip in blood pressure three days ago and he did a few more tests in lying and standing position and seemed satisfied, but deigned to offer a medical reason for the low blood pressure.

I asked him what had happened to our post-discharge support as defined in the notes. He checked the notes and the support was listed, so we should have had it. He said he would mention it.

Big Deal!

What good is that after the event?

I had a few more questions primarily for the Consultant and our keen young houseman asked if he could possibly answer them.

Well, it was hilarious.

I asked about Margaret flying because our youngest son lives in the States and it was a long way for her to swim. He obviously missed the point because he said it was all right for Margaret to fly and was she experiencing difficulty swimming?

I started to explain but Margaret interrupted me with a halting, 'Oh, that's just one of my husband's jokes'. I could hardly contain myself.

Next I asked about driving a car.

The houseman did some more tests - mainly for peripheral vision and pronounced her fit to drive!

Wow!

Since Margaret had difficulty comprehending instructions and could hardly tell left from right, I thought that was a bit premature.

My next question was about the future and would she be on tablets for the rest of her life. We discussed the effects of the stroke and I described both the accident when Margaret hit her head on the pavement and the uncontrollable sickness that followed some twelve hours later.

The young doctor immediately realised the significance and said, 'Ah yes, that shows the cause and effect very well,' or similar words that meant the same thing. How I later wished that others had been so perceptive!

Margaret went to the 'Ladies' and so I wandered round looking at notices.

I found one that read 'Patient's Charter'. It listed all the things we had not had as 'promises to do'! I should send a copy to someone in authority (such as an administrator) and demand an explanation. There seemed little point in stirring up a hornet's nest at this stage and it would only upset Margaret, so I left it as it was.

We did see Dr Olds then, who reiterated his opinion that recovery as far as it was going would take three years. He estimated that my wife would make a ninety to ninety-five percent recovery during that period.

Events to date bear out that hypothesis. This Consultant was up to the minute and on the ball in the style of the famous Cardiff geriatrician, Professor John Pathy - a personal acquaintance of mine for many years until he died.

John Pathy is a revered name in Cardiff medical health circles. He held the first Chair in Geriatric Medicine ever granted by a University and his work on elderly patient rehabilitation was respected worldwide. His main theme was 'whole of body' medicine, a policy that is vital for those people who were over 50, say.

This ideology implied that any geriatric changes were just as important to deal with as other more routine complaints. Neither ailment must suffer just because you were old.

We left the Clinic with an appointment four months ahead.

In March, the speech therapy recommended by Geraint Olds was actually started.

Some of the sessions were not good. There was that particular picture that was used for analysis. Margaret was supposed to interpret this line-drawing that had been photocopied too many times. Even I had difficulty in understanding what was required.

My wife grew to hate that bad photocopy picture and would often break down and cry whenever it was brought up in conversation. I think it was the same one that West Wing had used and that always seemed to upset her when she saw it in the hospital, or the copy I had obtained.

At home, we gradually progressed onto dictation and writing over the succeeding months and even today, we do some of these word exercises along with others that I have developed over time.

Some six years after the accident we were still keeping to the training schedule, adapting it and updating it as Margaret conquered the set pieces.

Amongst other things, I was qualified to teach adults and have taught blind, deaf and other handicapped people to use computers. Teaching Margaret everything from scratch stretched my patience and ingenuity to the limit.

Those same skills have however, had to come in useful for teaching my wife to read, write, do simple mathematics and comprehend.

The fact that the training took place every day at the same time each day, has had an enormous impact on my wife's recovery. At the Stroke Association meetings she attended once a week, Margaret met many people who might have benefitted from such regular training.

By mid-March, I realised that Margaret's physical ability and reflexes were almost back to normal. Because of her interest in the car, I gave her some driving lessons. After all, she still possessed a valid driving licence and insurance.

These lessons started in a super-market car park, funnily enough. I just asked her to park the car in another slot to see how she got on.

Margaret proved that she had not lost the ability to drive a car. The problem was that she could only drive to places she knew of since the accident and could then find her way back.

I asked her helper, Hilary to accompany Margaret for a drive just to check that my ideas were not based on euphoria or my presence. She did just fine.

One of the oddball TV medico-scientific programs gave me the clue to why and how Margaret had retained such motor skills following what was technically a stroke. The motor skills (nothing to do with a motor vehicle, but those skills that affect our normal movement reflexes such as tying our shoe laces, or writing a letter, say) are a separate function and often survive strokes and head injuries – or so I gathered from the program.

This driving in the car with Hilary was most successful and so Margaret was able to drive alternate weeks with her helper on trips to the Stroke Association.

Just to be sure, I asked Gethin Welland to arrange for the Disabled Driver Assessment Centre to put my wife through their assessment. He said that he would make an appointment for Margaret to be assessed at the local Driving Assessment Centre at Rookwood Hospital in Cardiff.

I wrote to DVLA Medical Section in Swansea, to bring them up to speed on what was happening. Maybe they would not require any further testing before allowing Margaret back on the road. At this precise moment in time, as they say, Margaret had not been banned from driving. Her vehicle insurance was up to date, so there was only me to prevent her from driving her car anywhere in the world if she so desired.

The 'driving skills' test all took some time to come through of course. Meanwhile, I let Margaret drive me on longer journeys and eventually, along the M4, extending the distance as her confidence grew. All the while I watched for signs of tiredness.

Our next visit to the GP surgery was productive. Dr Welland changed the hypertension pills to half-strength (I should probably say quarter strength because Margaret was now on a quarter of the standard dose.

We were very much aware that she might have been taking these pills forever and so any reduction in strength I saw as one step towards no pills at all.

Margaret hoped that she could lose the smell that pervaded her life at the moment. It was probably due to the pills. She could smell it on her clothes and on her body day and night and complained about it all the time. I had my sense of smell removed in my teens by overzealous ENT surgeons trying to remove my hereditary nasal polyps, so any strange smell was irrelevant to me.

Chapter Seven
On with the Litigation

The Claim against Cardiff City Council was progressing by courtesy of a Reading firm of Solicitors – Kennet, Newbury and Thorpe. Whilst the City Council had admitted liability, an independent medical examination was to be arranged for Margaret to assess the damage and the prognosis.

The Medical Examination.

This took place at the surgery of Dr X in Cardiff on Wednesday 19 April 2000 at 10am. Present were Dr X, Mrs. Margaret Greenridge and John Greenridge, (spouse).

On 19 April 2000 at 10am, we attended the Surgery of a semi-retired neurologist who had been retained by both parties' Solicitors to carry out the medical examination.

The surgery was dark and dismal as I recall and the desk had numerous papers scattered over it. The guy was dealing with more than one Case, I assumed, but I may have mis-interpreted those several piles of papers.

The nominated medical specialist for the examination asked for an account of what had happened so far. Dr X was then apprised of the full history and circumstances of the accident and the subsequent hospitalisation and convalescence.

Margaret and I were then asked for some background details relating to her family medical history - in particular, parental age on death. So you can imagine my surprise and dismay to discover that, in his Medical Report, Dr X managed to get some of these details wrong.

After the usual testing of Margaret's reflexes, I let slip to the doctor about the left/right foot problem and he made Margaret walk a straight line. Somehow from this observation, this neurologist was able to confirm the right/left foot problem in his Report. Amazing!

However, the problem was not physical, as Dr X appeared to think. It was mental – a result of the damage to Margaret's brain as anyone but Dr X might have deduced. Dr X should have been trying Margaret out on '*The Hokey Cokey*', or something similar.

You know!

'*You put your left foot in,*

You put your left foot out.

In-Out, In-Out and shake it all about.'

Then the mental problem of selecting the correct foot would have been obvious to even a blind consultant.

I began to get bad vibes.

Dr X carried out a series of tests after this but did not undertake a blood pressure test on Margaret. This omission we both found quite surprising in view of his later comments in the medical report.

We had a laugh about it in the car afterwards because Margaret had been worried that she would have to undress for such a test due to the tightness of the clothing she was wearing on her upper arms. I had reassured her that, since the guy was a doctor, it would be all right to remove her tight clothing for the examination. But it never happened.

The neurologist had used an ancient brass fundoscope to examine Margaret's eyes. What ophthalmologist worth his or her salt would use such an instrument these days, I wonder in order to ascertain precise information to forward to a Court of Law, (Quincy says). I was not impressed. I can recall my GP in the late forties of the twentieth century using such an instrument and it was old then.

The Medical Report was prepared by this ex-neurologist as evidence to be presented to a Court of Law so I expected it to be pristine. My time in the NHS had shown me the standard medical output for the Lancet and BMJ and other medical magazines – several of which I had contributed to, even though I have no medical degree or qualifications. But that is another story.

In the due course of time, as spouse, I received a copy of the Medical Report for comment. This Report was as presented by Dr X, Consultant Neurologist to the legal teams for onward transmission to the Court.

When I received this copy of the Report from our solicitors - Kennet, Newbury and Thorpe, I reacted badly.

After my NHS experience of the clear, concise and detailed reporting of consultant medical staff in the University Hospital environment, I considered that this Medical Report on Margaret was not good.

My initial reaction was that the Report had not received the attention due to a document that was to be presented to a Court of Law as evidence.

The mis-spelling of the medication (and we are all aware of the importance of getting the name of the medication correct) was an unacceptable error as were the errors of fact. The grammatical and typographical errors were merely cosmetic, but did nothing to endow confidence in the general accuracy of the Report - or in Dr X for that matter.

It was surprising, in view of the essential nature of evidence for Law, that no one associated with the production of the Report - not even the retainers, Y.Y Ltd - had taken the trouble to check the grammar, or the syntax.

This would be vital in my estimation, if only to ensure that the Report was understandable and adequate if not complementary to the perceived status of the writer - a medical doctor previously at consultant level. But, I would bet that few other lay people would take such trouble as I did with a report from a semi-retired doctor previously at consultant level!

The Report lacked that professional polish I would have expected of consultant-level medical staff reports in my experience and certainly would confuse the Court in some parts of the dialogue. Was it thus designed, I wondered?

My initial reaction was not to make too much fuss since, after all, it was '**THE**' Medical Report. When I rang our appointed Solicitor, Mr Thorpe, he told me that the Report was ready to go to the Judge in the Civil Case.

I was appalled.

I would not have given six out of ten for the English. Well, maybe just a few more than '*nil pointes*', as the French say.

I decided to point out a couple of the obvious errors but became aware that certain parts of the Report - relating to blood pressure and a pre-existing hypertension condition - could not possibly be true as far as my wife's health was concerned. If those comments were true then there had been some serious negligence on the part of my wife's GP and her Optometrist, not to mention the NHS doctors who treated her during her convalescence.

I discounted this possibility on a basis of my knowledge of both Dr Welland, Margaret's GP, plus the current GP Surgery policy on high blood pressure. Then there was the professional standing of Iris Oglvie, Margaret's Optometrist, at least within Wales if not the UK.

The glaring feature that really upset me was that Dr X appeared to totally ignore the circumstances of the accident and the contribution of the paving to Margaret's trip. Perhaps he did not have the value of the similar circumstances of the trip and fall of the Scottish Secretary, Mr Dewar, to guide him!

My wife and I had recently heard of a forty-year-old lady who tripped and hit her head while on a walking holiday in Austria. She died, as did Mr Dewar, possibly because both were being treated with an anti-clotting drug called warfarin. Maybe warfarin-takers should wear crash helmets!

Fortunately, because there was nothing wrong with Margaret's blood pressure - or anything else as it happens, there was no reason for her doctor to prescribe warfarin prior to the accident. Otherwise, she could have ended up with a similar result.

To add credence to what I have inferred, I had been told by Margaret's Hospital Consultant that, following the brain-scan examination after the accident, the diagnosis written up in the hospital case-notes indicated that this was a post-trauma case and not a hypertensive stroke such as was quite obviously assumed by Dr X.

In direct contrast to Dr X's interpretations, the inference imbued by the hospital diagnosis meant that the brain damage was due to the fall and not due to the condition of Margaret's cardio-vascular system failing. (Due to a heavy blow fracturing a normal healthy pipe - well, blood vessel, then - as opposed to the bursting of an aging worn-out pipe!).

Why did this not appear somewhere in the Report?

Surely that diagnosis had a bearing on the Case?

Dr X had access to the hospital records. It is almost as if he disregarded them in favour of his own hypothesis.

Further to that, Margaret's post-accident condition was not that of a typical stroke patient (if there is such a thing). There was no left side paralysis, no salivary drip from one corner of the mouth, no loss of swallow and no facial palsy.

Margaret could talk fairly normally from the start of her recovery. It was only her memory that had suffered in the end. I believe they call it amnesia if you lose your memory following a blow to the head, but this word was never used in my hearing. Perhaps it has gone out of fashion in medical circles.

Fortunately, the Third Party in the Case accepted the trip circumstances. I think it was largely because there was good evidence for stepping on a paving that tilted, scoring and taking the chrome off one shoe to a depth of two inches and compressing the toe of the following shoe in the recovery attempt. My several photographs of the state of the pedestrianised street may have helped after all.

The outer clothing worn by my wife also provided key evidence. Her clothing was dirtied with sand and mud from a fall on what should have been fairly clean standard city paving blocks under normal circumstances. Anyone could observe the sand and mud as it squirted up from beneath the pavings by the passage of vehicles along the pedestrianised lane. It was more noticeable after rainfall.

The sand, together with subsoil clay, was both present on Margaret's coat, giving a clear outline of the joints of the paving.

Thus one can deduce that there must have been huge gaps in the pavement underpinning, causing the pavings to tilt when stepped upon. (Says TV's Dr Quincy! Ok, so I watch too much television!).

Dr X's hypothetical idea - of my wife possibly having a stroke unrelated to the fall - had to have some clinical evidence of at least a likelihood of the event occurring. In other words, it should have been substantiated and supported by details from Margaret's previous medical history in order to suggest that as a possibility. So Dr X invented the phantom hypertensive retinopathy that no one else could find either before the accident or subsequently.

There were available for all to see, several historical records of Margaret's blood pressure taken over the previous twelve months. These were all within normal limits.

In this respect then, it was only Dr X's phantom blood pressure readings and the eye examination with his ancient brass fundoscope that supported the idea of the hypertensive state as the major cause of the accident. Added to that were the elusive hypertensive retinopathy of the eyes that no one else has found in the ten post-accident years to date!

(Maybe we should have looked at Dr X's other recent Cases. Perhaps there was someone he examined who had such a condition and who had been passed by Dr X as 'normal').

This neurologist appears to have ignored the medical records, my wife's general health records and her current lifestyle to accomplish his hypothesis.

Dr X's hypothesis just did not hold up. Consider the instant recovery of my wife as she was helped up by two members of the public (despite a severe blow to the head). Then, her personal decision to rest for an half-hour before proceeding. These were key pointers.

The uncontrollable sickness and the brain haemorrhage some twelve hours later gave good cause and effect - all points ignored by Dr X in his Report, but commented on by other medical staff involved in the case. Did the man discount a whiplash type injury to the brain, which is the more likely scenario?

Fortunately, the admission of liability by the Third Party gave some perspective to the incident. The photographs of the accident site lent support to the idea of the actual trip. The street was a pedestrian nightmare at the time and the City Council were obviously aware of the situation to admit liability in the face of Dr X's damaging Medical Report.

Queries to Dr X about the content of his Medical Report and the unsupportive nature of his 'facts' were inevitably rebuffed, ignored, or went largely unanswered. The quoted blood pressure readings were proved to be fictitious - even Dr X could not find a reference for his quoted values. His desperate attempt to use 'post-accident' details to get himself out of a hole was criminal in my estimation.

Since the issue of the Medical Report, the hypertensive retinopathy has not been confirmed by any of at least six other medical doctors, nor two independent eye-specialists, under both routine fundoscopy using modern equipment and full eye-pupil dilation. We are talking about examinations covering some nine or ten post-accident years here!

I asked my wife's doctor to check her eyes and he could find nothing. On our next visit to see Iris Oglvie, Margaret's Optometrist dilated her eyes and did a full scan of her eyes for any possible changes and found nothing.

That lady then asked her brilliant young colleague to carry out an independent full examination of the eyes while they were dilated and that optometrist found nothing either.

Iris Oglvie was prepared to put her reputation on the line that there was no stage 2 hypertensive retinal changes present in my wife's eyes. This was supported by her colleague, Tim Sewell.

My wife was due for her final visit to see Geraint Olds on June 13th and he himself decided to do some fundoscopy but he could find nothing. He reiterated his opinion as to cause and effect as per his original diagnosis.

Further, during the previous three months, I had my wife's eyes examined for field-of-vision testing on two occasions by different doctors - one manually and the other using one of the new electronic testing systems - in order for her to take up driving a car on the highway again. Her eyes were rated with the top score!

In the meantime, Margaret had her eye-pressures checked for her glaucoma screen as well. None of this testing has shown up any defects - not even Grade 1 hypertensive changes.

This is despite her brain damage and subsequent hypertensive state - the latter that could be attributable to other known factors. Margaret's allergy to lactose would be one of those, since most of her medication was unfortunately lactose-based.

Alternatively, there might have been hypothalamus involvement following the severe memory loss. In view of Margaret's on-going reduction in blood pressure levels as the healing progressed - albeit with some help from the pills, the hypertensive argument did not hold up.

If all this sounds too technical or medical, don't give up just yet. All I want to do is to suggest that the guy got it wrong. Either the wrong medical notes from his desk, or the wrong interpretation of the facts. Dr X never did find any references to support his diagnosis and that says it all to me.

I wrote to Mr Thorpe expressing my concern and asked him to contact Dr X a second time to request details of the origin of the quoted high blood pressure reading of 180/100. I also asked the Solicitor to let Dr X know about the evidence of previous eye tests including those performed when my wife had the eye infection a few months prior to the accident - all for comment.

The response from Dr X was in my opinion a disgrace to him and his profession. It was pure flamboyant rhetoric and conflicted with the stated diagnosis in the medical records. He actually had the gall to reproduce the **Post-accident admission sheet** in support of his **pre-accident** medical assessment once again. Well, I ask you!

He made no attempt to give details of the other requested information to support his views. His response cast doubt on whether the information ever existed.

This left the 'OPINION' in the original medical report totally unsupported and open to question again.

And there was no mention in his Medical Report of the original medical treatment for the post-accident condition. It was given in the notes (Dr X's latest extract from the Discharge Summary - Item numbered *3. Orthostatic hypotension, medication: Amlodipine 5mg daily.'*). So I guess that initially at least, Margaret's blood pressure was lower than normal and not higher as asserted by Dr X.

What was critically important about this post-accident treatment was that it soon became necessary to effect a change in my wife's medication.

Margaret experienced some awful side-effects from that first drug used to combat the post-accident hypotension (low blood pressure).

In my view, this was a vitally important medical consideration where litigation was concerned. This was because of the distress that had been caused by the drug *'amlodipine'* during treatment. The treatment carried with it the possibility of lasting damage to kidneys, liver, lungs or heart were that treatment to have continued. And, I guess you now have a valid reason for my paranoia (or vigorous concern).

All the doctors I have spoken to about my wife's condition and her chance of recovery have volunteered the information that there was good correlation between the accident happening and the brain's haemorrhagic incident (the internal bleed) occurring twelve hours later. It is a classic scenario. Dr. X never even considered this aspect of the Case.

Several doctors involved in Margaret's post-accident treatment have even gone to the trouble of explaining to me about head injuries. I was told how an accident where the brain whiplashes backwards and forwards may result in the tiniest blood leak. It is this leak that spreads slowly through the tissue until it knocks out some function. Then the brain just switches the part off.

This help and advice given freely by medical staff, has been of enormous benefit to me as a deeply concerned Carer.

Back to Dr X's Medical Report, if you can stomach it. The entry relating to my wife's ability to understand what was said to her was quite wrong.

In actual fact, she had been able to get the gist of most of what was said to her from early on in her convalescence. Her problem was that she could not usually glean enough to understand the plot in a TV program. She could not translate from her brain to her mouth (aphasia). Nor could she easily interpret and rationalise two separate instructions.

This should have been clear from the Case Notes available to Dr X. For instance, I know that Margaret's Consultant used this unusual phenomenon to describe her condition to his colleague while he was carrying out a three-month post-accident check-up.

(We normally communicate in 'duplex' and so our conversation is two-way. Margaret's was basically one-way at a time, like the old aircraft communication system where you switch between receive and transmit. The question and answer appear as separate messages and this sometimes leads to unrelated communications. She used to hedge her answers, but after about a year, she could answer directly, given time).

You will see examples of Margaret's problem in world communication systems today. With satellite communication there is often a time-delay between the interviewer and the interviewee conversations. We have to wait for a response - a phenomenon that you will perhaps recognise from seeing live TV News reports over a satellite link.

It is this time-delay that makes understanding difficult and allows the thread of the news to be broken. Some of my wife's responses exhibited this time-delay and often, contact was broken if my wife could not find the words to express her response to a question as the listener became tired of waiting.

Examples were also apparent when Margaret went shopping. She would ask an assistant for something. If the assistant queried the size, or the colour or the price, my wife would be in deep trouble because her brain was incapable of translating the information quickly enough for a response. She usually clammed up and walked away frustrated by the experience.

On the other hand, in a supermarket Margaret had little problem since she could select the item she wanted at leisure. She then had time to sort out the money while the checkout person was processing the goods through the till.

The time delay between the transaction processing and the request for payment - money or plastic card gave Margaret enough time to respond without any trouble. The till-assistant never had the opportunity to pressure Margaret into an immediate response.

The admission of liability by the Third Party gave some perspective to the whole incident. The photographs of the accident site lent support to the actual trip as the cause of Margaret's brain damage. The street was a pedestrian nightmare and the City Council themselves obviously must have been be fully aware of the situation to admit liability in the face of Dr X's Medical Report.

As I mentioned earlier, repeat queries to Dr X about the content of his Medical Report and the unsupportive nature of his 'facts' have been rebuffed, ignored or largely unanswered. The quoted blood pressure readings were fictitious - even Dr X never ever discovered a reference for his quoted values. He got quite shirty over this.

An offer to re-examine had been ignored or declined (I am not sure what happened to the offer to re-examine, but it was not taken up, for sure.). The Third Party and our Solicitors jointly and unusually, then requested a second medical examination because of Dr X's intransigence.

The Report was of course, confidential and sub-judicae so there is no way that I could reproduce it here. Though my understanding was that it never got as far as the Courts. Our Claim was eventually settled, but I never received anything about a Court ruling, so it may have been settled out-of-Court.

What happened next was really a battle. The Neurologist had used post-accident data to back-up his Report on Margaret's pre-accident disposition. Some of the medical evidence could not be substantiated either from Margaret's Medical History, or from the findings of three or four independent specialists.

The short argument on that score was that I rang up the General Medical Council for advice.

In the end, it was Margaret's Solicitor, Mr Thorpe, who put the matter to rest. He hinted that the Court might rule that I had interfered with the Report. I was not medically qualified to comment on it even though my evidence was correct of fact and could be substantiated in every way. This was medical evidence and that was that, it seemed.

What I would like to do is to give you the bits that I personally researched that were at variance with the Medical Report. Here they are in summary.

Both Dr Olds - during Margaret's hospitalisation, and her Optometrist, Iris Oglvie, disputed the grade 2 hypertensive retinopathy discovered by Dr X. with his ancient fundoscope. My wife's optical history concurred with their dispute with Dr X's findings.

Previous to the accident, there had been several complete and exhaustive eye examinations under a variety of conditions (including eye-dilation) by doctors and by internationally recognised eye specialists covering the preceding twelve months.

Eye examinations were carried out at the GP night surgery and at the University Hospital Eye department when Margaret contracted a severe eye infection in the summer preceding the accident.

On top of this, Margaret was having regular eye check-ups for glaucoma screening because her mother had glaucoma.

It is difficult to contemplate that all these medical staff of vast experience – some of them specialist eye gurus - would have missed the early or intermediate stages of a hypertensive retinopathy, (something well within their field of expertise), or a high-value blood pressure.

Retinopathies were one of the things that those experts regarded as 'bread and butter'.

Perhaps Dr X does not eat butter!

As far as the hypertensive bit was concerned, all doctors throughout the United Kingdom now follow the new government guidelines for combating high blood pressure. So we golden oldies now take pills for high blood pressure whether we have it or not.

Regular check-ups are the norm for everyone. There is no way that hypertension could be missed as far as I could see in Margaret's case. The pre-accident blood pressure results were available, but Dr X declined to look.

Chapter Eight
My Comments on the Medical Report

Page One

The data given on Page One is accurate and is the only page of the document that displays this quality.

Page Two

In the paragraph on Social History, somehow or other the fact that my wife *'now takes Bendrofluizide tablets for her hypertension'* appears. The fact that she did not have hypertension prior to the accident is obscured by this wicked little ploy. The fact that the drug was only prescribed by Dr Olds when Margaret was hospitalized *after* the accident is significant.

The ex-neurologist inferred that the blood-pressure tablets were taken irrespective of the accident. In other words, he appeared to assume that she was hypertensive all the time and doctors have only now got round to treating her for the disease! That was a load of baloney.

This was not a true representation of the facts and perhaps a slight on her GP. Margaret's GP had thoughtfully printed out a graph for me of all the available blood-pressure data he had on file. There were no high readings that we could see.

So, my wife was not clinically hypertensive prior to the accident. The hypertension must have been induced by the damage to the brain. The first evidence of high blood pressure was given in the Hospital Admission Record and that was some eighteen hours post-accident. This was the document Dr X tried to pass off on me as pre-accident data and as stonewall proof of Margaret's predisposition for high blood pressure. What rubbish!

Further, the name of the drug used to combat the raised blood pressure was spelled incorrectly in the Report. However, it really formed no part of her pre-accident Social History because of the post-accident prescription!

One could also raise some questions about the construction of sentences and grammar if this report was to face a Judge in a Court of Law. The meaning of the text was not clear and concise and was (perhaps deliberately?) open to mis-interpretation. Certainly it was not typical of the level of English used by 'Consultant' grade medical staff in my experience over many years. I doubt it would pass the editor of the British Medical Journal, for instance.

There was much to quarrel with in the first paragraph under 'Circumstances of Accident' on Page Two of the medical report. This was because it was based on what can only be described as '**interpreted**' narrative.

This piece of mis-information was loosely based on Dr X's recall from the notes he had taken when he examined my wife. The only point I would like to make is that the accident was well described to Dr X. The only reason for Mrs. Margaret Greenridge's' trip and fall was undoubtedly the loose paving and that was obvious to us all - except Dr X.

The neurologist did not seek to examine the coat or the shoes nor did he examine the accident site. (Quincy). He just looked at my wife and decided that she had fallen maybe prior to, during or just after a haemorrhagic stroke. Nothing about the loose pavings' contribution to Margaret's trip in Church Street of course.

My wife spent up to thirty minutes in the Café following her trip over the paving. (She recalled that immediate rest for thirty minutes was one of my personal recommendations imposed on our two sons to be followed after a serious fall).

Then, she actually continued shopping for a while after her trip and subsequent rest in the Café. There were two receipts in her hand-bag for goods that are timed after the accident occurred! Dr X was informed of this fact but he seemed to have lost the point in his deliberations. If my wife had suffered a hypertensive stroke just prior to the accident, it is most unlikely that she would have been able to carry on shopping!

When a stroke happens to someone, people around the incident usually call for an ambulance and the person is immediately hospitalized. They are not able to go on shopping, or get on the bus, or drive the car, or any of the things Margaret did during the rest of the day. However, with an injury caused by a blow to the head, it is the slow weep of blood that eventually leads to the classical sickness and collapse within the next 24 hours.

So they say. But even you will be able to deduce that!

The vomiting described in the next paragraph should have been described as 'uncontrollable' - hence the urgent admittance to hospital. This also was a significant feature in the diagnosis of course. Omitting it allows for the diagnosis of pre-accident stroke rather than as a result of the blow to the head sustained in the accident – the latter that might be considered typical in most medical circles.

Page Three

The first sentence (referring to me, the spouse) is inappropriate as part of a 'Physical Examination' on my wife. Any such comment might possibly have been included under Social History. However, I was not part of Dr X's brief. My name should not have appeared in his Medical Report on my wife to be presented to a Court of Law.

Whilst the first two paragraphs in this section were not entirely correct, they were acceptable and actually managed to give the correct overall impression.

'Hurray!'

Dr X was given every opportunity to revoke the second sentence within the third paragraph (relating to the elusive retinopathy) but has resolutely or obdurately, declined to do so. This is in the face of stiff optical evidence to the contrary.

Since the examination, Dr X has not been able to support the non-existent Grade 2 hypertensive retinopathy he said he discovered in Margaret's eyes.

Photographic, ophthalmic, optometric and medical evidence from a wide variety of eminent practitioners indicated that Dr X's findings were not sustainable. Margaret never had such an eye disease according to everyone else who has repeated the examination. Nor has such a disease developed during the ten post-accident years.

Those organizations included the Eye Department at the University Hospital - who offer a far more reliable standard of examination than Dr X with his old-fashioned pre-WWII brass fundoscope. That hospital's Eye Department is equipped with all the latest microscopic eye-examination machines. Indeed, Geraint Olds and Margaret's Ophthalmologist, Iris Oglvie and her associate Tim Sewell use the same or similar equipment.

Despite this, Dr X continued his futile search for evidence to support his findings to the point where he has twice produced false evidence to date. I have been able to refute this evidence because it is false and unsustainable, being largely post-accident data rather than the historic facts he needed to verify his statement.

Under the heading 'Opinion', contrary to the views expressed by Dr X, it seemed so logical to me for anyone in their right mind to assume that the *'technical details of her stroke'* **were** *'really relevant to the matter'*.

A haemorrhagic stroke following twelve hours after a significant blow to the head might almost be expected in someone over sixty. It showed good correlation between cause and effect according to some of the Hospital doctors who examined Margaret in her recovery state. Even Dr X came to that conclusion in the next paragraph of his Report in direct contradiction to his earlier comment.

The second paragraph under the heading 'Opinion' was just a bit of fanciful hyperbolic conjecture and had no basis in fact. Nor to my understanding, was most of the Report tenable in the light of current medical thinking and practice on the subject of strokes and recovery prognoses.

The comment that *'Mrs G. was clearly a candidate for a haemorrhagic stroke, being hypertensive (180/100)'* has not been supported by any medical facts obtained from her GP records or the few hospital records. So, Dr X was not able to verify any pre-accident hypertension although he tried various devious ploys to achieve this aim since this 'anomaly' was brought to his attention.

Dr X even tried to pass off to **ME** - with all my NHS experience - the unheaded Hospital Admission Sheet as a pre-accident document because it showed a possible hypertensive state. Fortunately, the document carried a post-accident date, or he might have got away with it.

Well, they don't yet have a system for admitting people to hospital before they have the accident as far as I know. However, if you read my Sci-Fi novel about the 'time dimension', then you may come to the conclusion that it might become a possibility in the future.

Meanwhile, Dr X declined to pursue my suggestion that the hypertension was due to the post-accident concurrent damage to the hypothalamus that, amongst other things, controls blood pressure. I read about this somewhere in my investigations but failed to realize its significance at the time. I therefore omitted to obtain chapter and verse sadly. Well, I'm not qualified to judge such things.

If Dr X made a reasonable error of judgment, he was given every opportunity to declare it. All he achieved was to destroy my wife's confidence in justice. It was fortunate that Margaret was surrounded by some very reliable, astute and caring members of the medical profession. Those people enabled her to maintain her positive progress on the long trip back to health. I saw this as a vital commodity in the scheme of things.

Dr X failed to comment on the positive effects of the change of drug on my wife's blood pressure. Also, ongoing treatment for the hypertension had been largely scaled down as brain-function improved with Mrs G.s' ongoing recovery. Indeed, having spelled one drug name incorrectly, the guy totally omitted to mention the initial Amlodipine treatment for low (not high) blood pressure and the drug's known side effects.

Studying the daily blood pressure records I kept at home, I formed the opinion that some of the hypertension was most likely due to the use of the drug to which my wife responded adversely. Certainly her blood pressure dropped **up to ten points** as soon as the medication was changed to a drug that did not contain the lactose to which my wife was allergic!

This indicated to my untutored brain that, because the original drug had a lactose base, this factor might well have actually **induced** some of the raised blood pressure. (Up to ten points on the Systolic, if my records are anything to go by!).

Dr X was not aware that the retinal photographs taken a year or so later would dispel one of the major factors that he said supports his pet theory of a retinopathy. I have copies of Margaret's inner-eye photographs as a screen-saver on my computer! Even a novice can see that there is no retinopathy. (Little red spots all over the retina).

And, as you may have guessed, these pictures confirm that Dr X was wrong again. The retinal photos - taken as part of a normal eye-screen for glaucoma and nothing to do with the accident - showed no retinal changes at all.

My wife did not have - and was therefore not being treated for blood pressure problems prior to the accident. So she survived the blow. Hence the clot that damaged her brain probably saved her life. According to my unethical opinion of Dr X's medical report therefore, there is not much in it that would stand careful medical or scientific scrutiny.

I should have been less considerate of the people who treated my wife so wonderfully. I should have taken up the case with the General Medical Council. However, that was not in my nature. Also, I would endeavour not to use such a ploy even as a last resort while the medical profession were under so much pressure from the press because of a few rotten apples in the barrel.

End of comments on Dr X's Medical Report on Mrs Margaret Greenridge.

Chapter Nine
Almost a comment too far

Ok. So I made a meal of that. But, you can see that I did my best to put it all right as far as I was able. It was tough going with all the other things I had to do for Margaret.

Things progressed.

I was so disgusted with Dr X's performance that, as I said earlier, I did ring the General Medical Council with a view to asking for a full investigation, citing mis-diagnosis and subsequent intransigence as my reason. Then I realised that this would involve all the people who had given of their time and talent to save my wife from death and to improve her prospects for recovery.

I may still send my 'non-medical' comments up to the General Medical Council for vetting of course. I had to bear in mind that several of the people who had worked so hard on Margaret's behalf as well as friends and family, might come under close scrutiny. This would be most unfair.

Also, at the time, there were several high-profile cases including the Shipman case and the Liverpool and Bristol Hospital scandals about the unlawful removal of organs from babies who died in hospital - and the subsequent storage of those body-parts for further examination by certain hospitals. Medical men were seriously under fire. I have some good friends and acquaintances in the medical profession, one of whom is my wife's GP.

Doctors were being struck off right left and centre as they say. It was not a good time to heap coals on such a fire just because I felt that some neurologist had got it wrong even if it was my wife's Claim that was at stake.

I remain one of the dwindling number of people that still retain a huge respect for our NHS. The fact that it has been ruined by spending money on the large number of parasitic administrators instead of professional staff, is the only thing that needs to be addressed, Prime Minister.

Margaret's Consultant, Dr Olds, and her Optometrist, Iris Oglvie as well as her GP, Dr Welland all wrote letters supporting the case. I cannot tell you what they said in their respective letters, but that brought an end to my campaign. There was no point in my trying to get my point across if the combined weight of these three specialists did not put the matter right.

I eventually agreed that the original Report should be submitted, *warts an' all*, in the hope that the Judge would be able to compare Dr X's misjudgment of the situation with the reality presented by the three letters – one from Dr Olds who cared for my wife and the others from my wife's Optometrist and her GP.

I suspected that my best weapon was going to be the fact that my wife continued to improve past Dr X's proposed deadline for such advance. That alone must say a whole chapter about his lack of modern medical experience even though stroke recovery is all well-documented in the medical literature I have been able to read.

This was a silly situation, I know, when the whole issue could have been rectified by a second simple fundoscopy to rule out the hypertensive retinopathy hypothesis put forward by Dr X. I always suspected that he might have got the papers on his desk muddled and perhaps gave information from another patient. It happens.

Don't forget, Dr X has never been able to substantiate those figures he quoted and has several times tried the trick of using post-accident figures to dig himself out of a hole. Any doctor who does that should be dis-barred in my opinion and certainly held in contempt. But I guess it goes on sometimes as dubious hypotheses need supporting evidence.

I am now fully aware of the crass stupidity of my actions in the light of future events. Hindsight is the next great breakthrough in technology and hopefully, we shall all reap the benefit of it.

All my technical shouting and posturing made no difference in the end and may well have damaged my wife's Case if it had come to open Court.

'Learned Counsel' would have torn my unqualified comments to shreds and we may even have lost the Case because of it. The Law is outside the reality of life as we live it and bows to life as it may variously be interpreted by 'legal experts', or according to past precedent and prejudice. I already knew this to my cost from previous attempts to obtain redress for other sins committed against me.

Gethin Welland, my wife's GP in our local Surgery is first rate. He has supported Margaret through her recovery and has adjusted treatment in line with her progress.

I have tried to have the hypertension treatment stopped in view of the good blood pressure statistics, plus Margaret's allergy to the lactose in the medication. Both Dr Olds and Dr Welland agree that she should continue for a while yet – if only to maintain the Government's initiative on Health Care for the elderly.

Chapter Ten
Back to Driving Again

It was Dr Welland, Margaret's GP, if you recall, who arranged for Margaret's driving skills to be checked amongst other things. He is a great guy.

In the due course of time, Margaret attended the Disabled Driver Assessment Centre for a four-hour test - far more stringent than the usual half-hour given 'Learner Drivers' to pass the Driving Test. If all prospective Driving Licence holders had to pass such a test then there would be a lot less bad drivers in the Country.

There was a problem that was high-lighted by the Assessment. Margaret's post-accident simple brain could only hold one instruction at a time. When she was asked to turn left at the next junction and then turn right at the intersection, she would do the first action impeccably and then drive straight on instead of undertaking the next action.

For the Assessment, she went out in a strange car with dual controls. So there was not even the privilege of driving her own car as a help. The Driving Instructor occupied the front passenger seat and the back seat held a specialist Clinical Psychologist lady.

On the journey down a dual carriageway, Margaret set her right winker going in order to overtake some slower traffic.

The Psychologist shouted about a lorry in the outside lane that came charging down the road like the proverbial bat.

The Driving Instructor had seen the lorry coming and had put his foot on the brake pedal to stop Margaret from moving into the path of the lorry.

He was too late.

Margaret had already slowed and turned back in, cancelling her winker as she did so. The instructor turned his head to face the Psychologist and just said, 'She was ahead of me and had it all under control!'

End of story!

The recommendation was that Margaret should take a couple of refresher lessons to try to iron out her little memory problem.

The first lesson was a constant battle to try to get Margaret to remember the second instruction. On the next occasion, Margaret took the initiative and said to the Instructor, ' I will drive you to all the places I visit in and around Cardiff, if you like.'

He agreed and so Margaret gave the man a Cook's Tour of Cardiff by driving to our Church, to the Stroke Association, to the Hospitals she attended, the Floral Club and the Gardening Club and Supermarket. At each place, she carefully parked in one of the parking bays before driving on to the next place.

The instructor was then fully satisfied with Margaret's driving ability.

Anyway, she was declared fit to drive and has driven herself around locally ever since. DVLC ask for a check on Margaret's 'field-of-vision' whenever she has her licence renewed, but she has always been well up on the required standard on that score.

She still lacks the confidence to undertake the longer journeys she would normally plan for herself and her friends on trips associated with her interests.

Margaret's general skill in other key areas continued to improve, being taught to cook, knit and sew by her friends and neighbours just like it was in '*The Patricia Neal Story*'. For a while, she still lacked the confidence to plan in those areas - a previous strong point.

My wife also had difficulty with comprehension and consequential planning and so stuck firmly to what she learned for the most part.

Even today, Margaret still experiences some difficulty with numerical calculations and cannot estimate say a half pint or a couple of ounces. Fortunately, our telephone displays people's names rather than numbers, so that she has no difficulty in phoning a friend.

Her lack of comprehension is most notable in our huge garden where planning for the seasons is vital to maintain the garden in tip-top shape. There are hundreds of specimen plants in the garden. The addition of Sandy, the gardener, was a boon to her horticultural activities.

In the winter and spring, the greenhouse and carport are normally stuffed with the more delicate plants, seedlings and cuttings for next season. Thus the hiring of a gardener for one or two mornings a week has helped Margaret to make something of her former gardening skills.

As far as floral art is concerned, I think my wife will never recover that essential quality that singles out the good from the amateur, but she tries hard all the time.

The same is true in the kitchen. Before the accident, my wife won the Cup for her cakes, scones and biscuits and was always dabbling with new recipes. Now, the only way she can achieve these things is if I read out the recipe and help her to weigh out and measure the quantities.

Even then, we ate a proportion of food that had been over-cooked - or even burnt at the edges - for a while, or things with some essential ingredient missing. This is because she would forget to put the timer on, or forget that the food was still cooking, or failed to read one of the lines of a recipe.

Until she gained more confidence in her ability, she continued to need support for her endeavours. My wife has periods of depression since the accident and these I understand, are symptomatic of her brain injury. If she were a man, these depressive bouts would plague her life, so she is lucky in that respect.

Marital relations are foreign to her. Although I believe that she has learned to regard me with some affection, a lot of this is due to the fact that I always try to manage to be there for her when she needs me.

This is a long way from the loving couple that were the delight of our friends and the envy of many. It is not too long since friends travelled from all over Britain just to have lunch with us on our Golden Wedding day.

We have always been a couple and have always done things together since we were married. It is the same now, but for different reasons.

No one seemed too interested in how the accident occurred - a necessary evil to prove negligence in my opinion. The protagonists were merely interested in settling it as an insurance risk. When they agreed, then that was that.

For instance, out of the blue, in order to assess Margaret's abilities since the accident, an appointment was made by the Solicitors with an independent psychologist in Bristol – of all places. Were there none locally in Cardiff, capital city in Wales?

Bristol is one of the most difficult cities for us to reach from Cardiff since we find ourselves unable to walk on water. It lies immediately opposite Cardiff in the County of Avon, just about four miles away over the Severn Estuary. The road distance by comparison is 40 miles and includes the Severn Bridge toll-crossing, at least three different motorways and a convoluted drive through the Bristol suburbs.

We duly turned up at the appointed place that was not far from Bristol Zoo. Fortunately, I knew the general area quite well, having stayed for a week in digs once when I was on a pre-exam course.

The outcome was that Margaret was diagnosed as being too dependent on me for her own development to proceed!

Surprise, surprise! If we had been given all the prescribed help, this would never have happened!

A few sessions with a Cardiff psychologist were arranged in order to put the matter right. I had to pay for those, of course. A further insult - to my purse if nothing else!

I was not too hurt, or even taken aback at the findings, since they merely reflected the lack of input into Margaret's recovery by the Social Services and the NHS.

I was the only resource available to my wife. Yet, despite the lack of other support, Margaret managed to improve at a remarkable pace (notwithstanding Dr X and his now out of date prognosis). She still remains a very popular person and attracts attention wherever she goes.

Everyone who knows what happened notices and has commented on the upward surge in my wife's ability. We are now well past the period of recovery offered by Dr X and his 'diminuendo' theory whatever that was. Anyway, like the rest of his report, it bears no resemblance to the reality of the situation.

Perhaps I should have alerted Dr X at the time of his examination, to Geraint Olds' three-year prognosis. I believe Dr Olds forecast concurred with findings on similar cases that have been published in current medical literature. In any case, I shall continue with Margaret's retraining for as long as it takes.

'Plateau' status is the one big difficulty for stroke patients as with all education. But I know all about 'plateauing out'. (Okay, I know the word may not exist and I should have structured the line differently, but you know what I mean!) and have plans to cope with it.

It would be possible for me to continue in this vein since I have some 150 or more pages of diary entries to illustrate the progress my wife has made in the early years. There is however, enough in this verbiage so far to paint the picture of my wife as she was before the accident, as she has developed up until two years after the accident and what she will be like after the three years projected by Geraint Olds.

You should now be able to tell the good guys from the bad guys - those I have every confidence in and those I would avoid like the plague by virtue of their performance to date. My wife is fortunate to have had such a marvellous Consultant plus the benefit of our family and friends, her optician and her GP, who have been so caring in support of her recovery.

At this stage of my writing, I would like to pay tribute to those who were not close friends or family or hospital, but who have also contributed much to my wife's recovery.

These are our wider circle of friends throughout the country and the neighbours. Then, there are the people who run the Stroke Association and the helper they assigned to my wife. Also, there are those local friends who offered lifts and anything else that might be needed.

Next, there is the gardener, who has brought so much joy to my wife by her efforts in the garden and her general conversation. Then the people at our Church who have remembered my wife in their prayers and given her such a welcome back into the fold.

In contrast, the Social Services and patient support services have been conspicuous by their total absence. No follow-up after coming out of hospital - nothing. The only thing the Cardiff Social Services supplied was a questionnaire when they did a survey of the services they currently provide to the public at large, (except us, of course). I could have done without that.

I did apply for financial benefit help to pay for Carers and the like. The lady who came to do the assessment of need took one look at our lovely house and immaculate garden and I very much expect that this was why it was refused despite the fact that we are both on pension. On the other hand, perhaps I applied for the wrong thing in the first place.

My lovely computer business was the only major casualty and I still miss it. With the right support from the Social Services, this would not have been necessary.

I have not found a way of parting amicably with all the computer software. Some of the hardware was given to friends and acquaintances. The rest eventually went to the recycling section of the City tip, as they say. Well, computer stuff is all out of date in no time at all these days, so it becomes worthless very quickly. I still have all the books in my office library. Some are probably of historic value now.

Chapter Eleven
As good as it gets for stroke patients?

Getting back to the mundane, my new computer arrived a couple of days ago. It was now unpacked and the boxes stowed away for the future. I would have to spend some time setting it up. I couldn't wait with the excitement it generated, but would have to.

There was so much to do.

With Margaret still recovering from her accident, I really needed a plan of campaign.

Three more letters went out in the evening post and then I wrote a further one. But that missed the evening collection from our local post-box. That's eight or nine letters today.

I found myself looking forward to Tuesdays and the gardener now, because I could have some precious time to myself.

The gardener came with her cheery smile and Margaret retired with Sandy to the sanctuary of the greenhouse while I sorted out our broken microwave decision - based on a potential quote for £120 to repair the existing model and over £300 to replace it with a new Neff microwave.

The new Council Tax bill arrived first post. (Do we get second post these days?). Our bill was now over the £1000 for the first time. We pay by direct debit so I needed to do nothing. The Bank would see to it all.

The cost of living in the City of Cardiff – as elsewhere - has gone up by leaps and bounds these last few years through Poll Tax, Community

Charge and now Council Tax. Despite our age and our pension, we do not qualify for Benefit or a reduction.

We had to renew Margaret's tablets and eye-drops. A quick trip to the GP Surgery to pick up the prescription gave us the opportunity to go to Sainsbury's across the Car Park from the Surgery. The Pharmacy was right next door, so that was quite convenient for redeeming the prescription.

Margaret drove - both ways. My big car was a handful for her and the gears were different to her four-speed box in the VW-Polo. Since we intended to dispose of her car, I have encouraged her to get used to my car.

Tuesday evening was the Flower Club Charity Night.

The Club support local charities with an event once a year.

Unfortunately, because the adverts had not appeared in the local papers, the numbers were down and consequently the 'take' was down as well. The Flower Club had decided this year to do something for the Stroke Association in view of Margaret's experience. Pity about the reduced 'take'!

Meanwhile, I popped over to Cwmbran to continue our bowls team's quest for glory. Needless to say our fortunes rested on the last bowl of the match. However, in line with everything else at the moment, it seemed to be inevitable that we lost after doing well early on in the game.

Margaret woke up next morning with a deep cough and a few fits of sneezing. She probably caught a bug or some allergen at the Flower Club meeting. I left her to look after a runny nose as I went to my next computer class.

The run down the Vale of Glamorgan to Cowbridge to one of my few remaining computer classes was wonderful. It was dry and slightly frosty with a clear sky and not much traffic. The computer students were very enthusiastic.

I did so enjoy going down into the Vale of Glamorgan. I was going to miss it all when I was eventually forced to give up.

The Education Authority staff at 'Old Hall' at the west end of the town were all so very friendly. The place may have lacked the positive aura of the big city but despite the cutback in budgets, the staff were always very go-ahead and they managed.

After lunch at home, Margaret and I went looking for microwave ovens.

Sadly, the range of domestic microwave ovens that do not sport extras such as grills or kitchen oven facilities, was limited. We took notes on a couple of likely candidates in the £80 - £120 range. As it turned out later, none of these were suitable for building into a housing because of the fire risk.

I agreed to go into town with Margaret on Thursday morning to try looking in the big stores for microwave ovens. I was at that stage totally unaware of the waste of our time because of the build-in factor. It was only when we got back to the electrical superstore we were in on Wednesday that we found out our error.

I casually asked about putting their microwave ovens in housings. The helpful sales assistant read us the bit in the installation instructions about needing up to sixteen inches clearance on the right-hand side where the generator was fitted. This would be impossible in our kitchen, since the current machine sits in a 'built-in' housing.

We still had some time to spare before my Thursday class so we popped into a couple of kitchen outfitters to look at build-in models. We settled on Neff again and I drove Margaret home in time for a welcome cup of coffee.

On the way out to my class, I rushed across town to Seawall Road where the Neff Agency stocked spares and gave service. The quote they gave me for a new microwave oven made my eyes pop a bit. My Scottish purse had a fit of the shakes, refusing to open. I said that I would take a rain-check.

After our hectic day, we retired early. We were now sleeping in separate rooms because Margaret's cold was getting worse.

After the Friday class next day, I rang Saga Electrical when I arrived home and was given a more reasonable price. The Microwave was to be delivered by the following Friday if all went well. Meanwhile, I had to develop an acceptable alternative way of making my coffee using the milk-pan. No making it straight in the cup as I usually do in the microwave oven.

All that time to milk-watch and then the extra washing-up to go with it. However did we manage before microwave ovens?

I was surprised to see a motor-scooter park across the front door of the porch. My letter cancelling the Care-worker, posted first-class two days previously, had arrived at its destination on Friday morning. The missive was too late to cancel the Care-worker visit, despite having a first-class stamp!

I think that the Post Office made an error because I had used the new first-class stamp now available. Alternatively, the Care Service perhaps, had not opened the mail in time to take action due to the usual manpower shortages.

This latter hypothesis is the more likely. The Care-worker they sent was being hired from another organization that occasionally supply them staff on a part-time basis. The lady came from up the Welsh Valleys somewhere and was not from Cardiff where our local Care organisation is based.

I have found it best to take the easy way out of such crazy situations. So, when I rang the Care firm's office. I said as much and that we would pay for the Carer as usual. Am I not magnanimous on such occasions, despite my Scottish ancestry?

The following day, we decided to give Saturday shopping a miss.

The weekend was one of those idyllic periods of long sunny warm, enchanting days of Spring. Margaret and I spent as much time as possible in the garden. Mainly tidying and preparation but I did manage to plant the seed potatoes and cover them with fleece.

My morning tuition for Margaret continued apace as we tackled numbers, letters, words and descriptions. That 'first letter' problem persisted. By this time, Margaret was really good at expressing her gratitude for the trouble I took to ensure her health and welfare.

Each morning and evening I still took her blood pressure and pulse and made sure that she had her tablets and eye-drops. I only did it out of love so she had no need to thank me at all. It has developed into something of a ritual for me and I was only too glad that I proved able enough to keep a check on things. Age does funny things to the memory.

Meals were proving to be less and less of a problem. We decided what to have for our main meal early in the day. We then raided the freezer or the fridge to assemble all the ingredients for cooking or heating-up.

We made quiche again this week and now have a varied selection of meals for each day of the week. These always included plenty of vegetables and we had fruit if there was no obvious pudding to follow the main course. We continued to take vitamin pills at least once a week. I know it says to take them every day but with our diet we would probably excrete most of what was in the pills anyway.

Margaret's speech and comprehension continued to improve, though it must be said that she still sounded a bit peculiar when answering questions or queries, as opposed to talking off the cuff. There were also plenty of instances of her being stuck for a word. Hitting the brick wall was something she now avoided by either changing the subject, or trailing off the conversation as people often do quite naturally at our age.

I was very pleased with how she coped with the terrible strain of not knowing, or understanding. Occasionally, I would still be caught out by her just standing, or sitting and waiting.

On those occasions, Margaret would be patiently waiting for me to realize that she had not the slightest clue how to proceed with whatever was on the agenda at the time. A bit like the TV when it is on stand-by and waiting for someone to switch it on, or select a channel to view.

We did all our shopping early on Saturday morning. This released the rest of the glorious day of sunshine to the sublime or more mundane activities such as the garden, (or, for me, watching the next round of the Six-Nations Rugby Championships).

Needless to say, Scotland were by now, right on target to win the wooden spoon due to the usual alleged blind-refereeing blunders and a strong Welsh Team defence.

We topped the day with fish and chips from Victoria, which was nicely washed down with home-made shandies.

Sunday gave us another day in the garden. I managed to slip in occasionally for a rest (more TV rugby) and finished off setting up my new computer.

We did some of our regular phoning before getting ready for Church in the evening. I managed to contact son No.1 and son No.2 within a few minutes of each other. Getting the timing right for these two calls was tricky. It had to be just before evening mealtime in the UK and just after breakfast in the US.

Chapel in the evening chronicled the third episode in the 175-year history of our Church. It never ceased to amaze me how half the congregation made a bee-line for Margaret at the end of the Service. Those who could not get near enough to speak to her personally collared me on the way out to whisper their little messages of hope and support.

My usual Monday client was away so I called on an old customer from way back who was experiencing some trouble with his ancient green-screen Amstrad 8256. I felt like a GP telling a patient (the computer) to take it easy, stay warm and don't try anything until you have warmed up. Few computers fail to respond to my gentle administrations and this one was no exception.

I promised my client that I would bail him out in an emergency if the old computer eventually gave up on him. The guy was no longer the bright secretary of the local Gardening Club eeking out his retirement with such work. His wife now needed a Carer to get her up in the morning and put her to bed in the evening. He was suffering from acute Carer's Disease and I know just how he felt.

There was no way of telling which of them would go first - him or the old Amstrad. They were both past their sell-by date. Any sudden surge in their circuitry could cause a crash.

If nothing else, this duo provided a visible and timely reminder of the frailty of mankind. My friend's house was set by the lake with beautiful views of swans, ducks and geese flying in and flying out throughout the season. The autumn of life had come for him and winter was not far behind from the look of my friend and client.

Back home, the rest of the afternoon was spent in the garden. The strawberry patch looked like it needed some green-fingered genius to sort it out if we were to enjoy the fruits in a few months time. My efforts would have to suffice, though.

My gardening is purely mechanical - turn the ground over, plant the seed, allow it all to grow (and add the odd bit of Growmore from time to time) then harvest. For some things like peas and beans, I also cleared the ground after cropping in case there is the opportunity for a winter crop. It helped to keep down the weeds and destroyed winter havens for slugs and worse.

Sandy phoned to say that her sister had arrived from Brighton for a change of scenery. She could either leave her at home on her own, or would it be alright to bring her over. This sounded like an opportunity for Margaret to practice her words and conversation on a complete stranger and so I agreed to her sister coming.

The three ladies had a good morning - hard work, good conversation and a happy ambience to the day.

It was only when they had gone that I thought it would be nice to have given our visitor a bottle of wine to say 'Thank you'. I must remember to drop one in later this week.

The strawberry patch looked good with my two afternoons of work. All the plants needed to get them going was some of our homemade compost between the rows. Not much more for me to do in the veg. patch until April now. I could sow some seeds in the greenhouse. Leave that for another day, eh?

I remembered to ring my sister to wish her many happy returns of her birthday.

As usual at five o'clock, I sped off down the M4 to Cwmbran. As I neared my destination my nerves started to jangle with expectation.

Was there really a match tonight?

I spotted my friend Mal as soon as I entered the Bowls Hall. He too looked puzzled. The game was listed but no rink was reserved.

It all became clear when we realised that the team we were to play did not exist because of some administrative ploy to separate the new groups of three teams with a blank line on the list. There was no Team 4, 8 and 12.

Straightforward consecutive numbering divided into groups of three and the groups separated by a blank line would have achieved the same objective without disturbing the sequence.

Thus the progression of the team-numbers would have been representative of actual playing teams. I was amazed at the bizarre system that had been utilized by the organizers. Administrators again!

Mal and I had a 'roll-up' since the rink was free. No point in having a 'Bowls Night Out' if you don't get to play the game!

Next day, Margaret had me print out a letter for her in big print. She then painfully but precisely reproduced the print on a 'Thank You' card for our Devon friends who sent flowers a few weeks ago.

By caring for the flowers and utilising bits and pieces from the various arrangements, Margaret's now latent skills had made the flowers last for three weeks. She had not lost all her former talent.

Next day would be my last early start for Cowbridge! Certainly until the new season of courses commences in September. Maybe I should give up courses now.

I used to do a Summer School down there in June but those days have long gone. When it is a question of Local Authority money then there is no competition for saving a few pounds here and there.

The cost of putting on a Summer School for a small country area must outweigh the service considerations. In Cardiff, the Summer Schools continue to attract large numbers and this makes even the fringe subjects a viable proposition - the 'weak being supported by the strong' sort of thing.

It was the day for the next Stroke Association meeting so Margaret took a bag of boiled sweets with her to put into the weekly raffle. When she returned home, she proudly if humorously threw the same bag of boiled sweets down onto the breakfast bar.

'There', she grinned, 'I won those in the raffle!'

I laughed at the sheer absurdity of the situation. Normally she always put her raffle prizes back in the pot for the less fortunate to win but decided to keep the prize on this occasion for the fun it generated.

There was a certain tightening of the reins in Margaret's general demeanour today that I had not noticed before. A certain assertiveness reminiscent of bygone days before the accident.

Suddenly I found her making decisions and asking me to do things in a more positive manner. Organising my day and my work. Hmm.

It didn't last long but I felt it was significant.

Thursday was going to be a tightly scheduled affair with all the trappings of nightmare.

The second advert for the VW Polo had spawned only one serious buyer who could only come at 10am in the morning. He worked nights. He wanted such a car for his wife to use as a second car.

On the phone, he knocked the price down the standard £100. That was catered for in the asking price. What could I do but accept?

Margaret was upset a bit now that her car was being sold. She bickered about the way I had handled the timing. This guy was coming at ten and we had made a hair appointment for Margaret for 10.15am. She had no idea of how it would all fit together. I would be going to town after picking her up from the hairdresser's and going straight on to my class.

Decision time.

I took her to the hairdresser's shortly after 9.30am and managed to get back home by 9.55am. Five minutes to spare.

Very good.

The buyer was right on time. He took one look at the car, paid the money in £20 notes, filled in the slip for DVLA, Swansea, jumped in and drove off.

All this without checking whether there was an engine in it or having a test drive.

I had every reason to feel confident in the car's performance so there would be no come-backs. I even remembered to give him the pullout radio. The radio was virtually brand new and had been stored indoors between trips for the last couple of years for fear of theft from the car like the pre-installed radio.

Anyone could break into a Polo saloon car with a screwdriver in those days as we found to our cost with the pre-installed radio.

The whole car-sale transaction took about five minutes start to finish and I was left holding a large bundle of twenties. A casual flick through revealed that I was 2p short if you calculate one standard deviation.

Okay. If you are not mathematical then, in other words, it was all there when I counted it.

By midday the cash was safely tucked away in the bank.

When I picked up Margaret, I had my little joke.

'You're a little bit carless today, dear.'

'Oh, you sold it then.'

She cottoned on straight away. I told you she had changed up a gear in understanding!

After my class, it was the usual rush to get back home, pick up Margaret and drive her to her Speech Therapy session.

The novice therapist exerted her authority today. She came over to me and asked me to stay outside for the first part of the session. I didn't enquire why.

After a while, she came out of the room again and told me not to pressure Margaret, or give her hints and starters for words like I normally do.

I smiled, realising that I must have been unconsciously interfering with their assessment of Margaret's progress. I was so used to giving the little prompts that I did not even realize that I was interfering with the assessments.

I said nothing about their pitiful little 40 minutes-a-week if we were lucky, as against my whole day, seven days a week, that I spent training Margaret in all the skills that were missing in her portfolio. The library had books on pronunciation and I used these to good effect – particularly the alliterative sections. (You know! '*The ragged rock ran round the round robin*', or some such nonsense).

Margaret had very little speech and comprehension when I started her training. By the time the speech therapy started she was quite coherent and capable.

Well! You know what 'professionals' are like with us gifted 'amateurs' – even if she was just a trainee.

And there was I with qualifications a yard long – but none in her field that were of any importance. You needed a long envelope to write to me when I was gainfully employed, just to get all my qualifications on the same line. Same goes for my job-title.

They mean well, though, these professionals. There are too few of them around these days. They have a job to do and more importantly, we were lucky to have them at all.

You will realise that I don't mention much about sleeping, washing or making meals. I tend to regard these as too mundane with all the other things going on. Perhaps I should give an illustration of just how we manage our day now.

In the morning, around seven am, one of us - always me for the first few months until Margaret got the hang of it – would make a cup of tea and bring it up to bed. I would then take Margaret's blood pressure and put her eye-drops in each eye. I entered the results of the blood pressure in the diary and then carefully folded up the cuff and tube and packed the unit back in its box.

Next, we either practiced numbers or letters, followed by comprehension (looking at a picture and examining what was happening). Then we examined any artifacts within the picture such as clouds, hedges and the like. After that, if Margaret was not too tired, we looked at words under a key letter of the alphabet - such as 'P' and practiced pronunciation of the more difficult words.

We followed that, if time permitted, or provided Margaret felt up to it, by giving verbal descriptions of animals or objects.

Initially this latter game was designed to find the name of the animal/object as quickly as possible on minimal information. However, we expanded the description to include as much detail as possible - which took quite a few minutes.

This helped Margaret with comprehension and links. It also helped to overcome the stumbling block where a word could not be found in the brain and Margaret hit the blank wall. By using other words to describe the object, she could continue with her conversation.

The positive difference in her conversation was encouragingly, quite noticeable by comparison with her previous efforts to communicate. Her degree of confidence had increased considerably.

Margaret had always been able to make her own breakfast (nothing cooked – just cereal, coffee and toast) following the training she received in the Stroke Unit. Consequently, there has never been much of a problem at home. Our lunch usually consisted of self-made sandwiches. Since Margaret ate toast for breakfast, she managed sandwiches for lunch with comparative ease.

So far so good.

It was the main meal of the day that caused the problems. We both liked variety and Margaret wanted to try to cook something different on most days. It must be a 'woman' thing.

Our evening meal therefore, provided the challenge. We have always reserved Saturdays as our fish and chip night, (a northern English custom, I believe) though occasionally it has been changed to a Friday if we were due to go out on Saturday evening. There are plenty of occasions when we made something and give the fish and chip shop a miss though.

The first thing we had to do was to make a decision early enough in the day so that we could get all the ingredients together.

Should we have soup? If so, was there any in the freezer? If not, have we anything available to make some soup?

Our selection of homemade soups included tomato, lentil, leek, celery, carrot and orange, mushroom, butternut squash, peas or vegetable.

We would wash, peel, chop, and slice away at the ingredients.

Margaret then fried off some onions and cooked some potato if appropriate. Everything went into the pot and was cooked, or whatever you do to soup.

I then came along with the hand-blender (which is a technical job, of course and therefore suitable for a man with my technico-mechanical skills) and occasionally sprayed the soup all over the place in the process of homogenising it. If we wanted smooth soup, it would then be sieved and returned to the heat until ready to serve.

Any excess soup left over after plating up was put into old margarine cartons. When this residue cooled, it would be labelled and dated (usually but not always, as we discovered when looking for soup in the freezer) and then put in the appropriate section of the freezer for another day.

At work, before she retired, Margaret used to do this sort of storage operation with her laboratory samples when they needed to be stored below room temperature. So it was a skill that was probably imbued into her after some thirty-odd years of her employment. I suppose that it is difficult to lose such an almost in-bred talent, due to it being mostly a mechanical skill.

The main course would be decided on the same system. What was available? We always had salmon steaks once a week, fresh fish once or twice a week if possible, quiche - that Margaret would make of course, omelettes - plain, cheese or mushroom and home-made fish-cakes.

When I was having a pizza, Margaret would choose from chicken or meat. Sometimes when I had salmon or fish, Margaret would have other meat dishes.

All these would be accompanied by at least three and often as many as five, or six vegetables. Our selection would usually include such things as potato, swede, carrot, broccoli, cabbage, cauliflower, home-grown string beans and peas from the freezer, leeks, mushrooms and onions - the latter two fried.

With quiche or other pie dishes, or fish-cakes, we would have frozen peas, or tinned baked beans. Then there might again be string beans that we had previously harvested from our garden and frozen down in small lots. We might also include peas from our garden similarly treated.

For our dessert course we quite often ate fresh fruit – bananas, apples, oranges, grenadines or similar, grapes, kiwi and other soft fruit in season. There were also rasps, strawberries, gooseberries, black and red currants all from the garden, frozen in bags and dated.

We might have melon as a starter instead of soup. Apple pie was my favourite for dessert, but it was getting scarcer in our house since the accident.

Alternatively, we might have leftover chocolate cake from cookery exploits, suitably garnished with chocolate sauce and cream, or ice cream. Or Margaret would make a golden sponge or similar with syrup and custard. It was surprising how quickly the breadth of her cooking skills had grown, considering how she had to be trained just to butter bread in hospital only a few short months ago.

When there was a set recipe, I read out and/or calculated the amounts for each item and then explained how it was to be cooked and in what sort of container. If there was an 'all-in' or easy-cook variation to a recipe, then that was the one I chose.

It may come as some surprise to learn that we ate what we cooked, so it must have been reasonably edible if that was the case. Even so, we both like beautiful food.

Margaret could no longer estimate amounts, or work out recipes or anything of that nature. This became a serious handicap to her cooking skills as she struggled to conquer food manufacture.

One of the funniest, most bizarre happenings during Margaret's convalescence was her referral to the Memory Clinic at one of the out-of-town hospitals. The clinic was based on the top floor of the old

Nurses Home. There was a telephone entry system where you gave your name and your appointment details before you were allowed in.

The access door clicked open and we climbed the stairs. At the top, we were directed to the Waiting Room that also served as a small kitchen.

People came and went with cups of tea or coffee and occasionally offered us the same.

Time went by.

On one occasion, a lady I recognized from the old days popped her head round the door, saw me and smiled. I smiled back, as you do, but thought nothing of it.

An hour later, I got up to find out what was going on, since we had by now missed our appointed half-hour of memory analysis.

My old acquaintance was apparently in charge of the place. She said that she assumed that I was the specialist looking after Margaret since she recognized my face and new that I was 'high-up' in the establishment. She was totally unaware that I disappeared off the NHS map some twenty-odd years previously and that my specialty was laboratory based!

So, no analysis, or memory training for Margaret was the end result. I think that the Unit should take some of their own medicine in order to ensure that this does not happen again with other people who may have been NHS at some time!

Friday, 24Mar00 - the last day of the last winter computer course - dawned with rain-showers followed by bright sunshine. I needed a haircut - not badly but *'thinking of buying a violin'* sort of length.

This was to be the big day for Margaret. She had invited ladies from the Church for afternoon tea. The list of people she had chosen would make your hair curl. None of the meek and mild churchgoers, yet not quite the power behind the pulpit either.

I arrived home for lunch after a very good final computer class and was ready for anything.

Oh, I forgot to tell you that there had been a phone call on the previous day confirming delivery of the new microwave oven between 7am and 1pm today. Also, our friend Ellen Rowe was coming over at 8.30am to help Margaret to make a big chocolate cake for the tea. They would make fresh scones as well - to be served with butter, jam and clotted cream.

All was well except that there was no sign of the promised microwave delivery. So much for advance warnings about deliveries.

After a shortened lunch break, I drove off to pick up four of the intended guests. The first one was not quite ready when I knocked her door. It took her a few minutes to get her coat.

There were road works at the junction with the main road. These were managed by temporary traffic lights. No lights for the side road though where I was bound. I was lucky and nipped round the work-area between light changes to get ahead of the waiting queue of cars.

I made good time down Northern Avenue before cutting across two minor estates to my second pick-up point.

No one at home.

Onto the third who was ready and waiting for us. Detour back to the second - still nobody at home! I phoned Margaret just to check that they had not arrived in their own car before making tracks for home.

Later, I phoned our two missing guests who had just got home from some hospital appointment. They had forgotten, or 'had a senior moment' about Margaret's afternoon tea invitation but had nothing pending so I got the car out again and retrieved them.

Well, it is a bit like that as you get older.

Let's face it. Memory is a precious commodity and, like gold dust, there is very little of it around when you most need it.

I reminded Margaret's two friends that I had personally collared them in Church on Sunday evening to invite them. I had given precise details of time and place and also that I would be picking them up.

Neither had any recollection of the event.

Sad, isn't it.

They could end up winning the lottery and forget to cash the cheque.

It was an enjoyable and hugely successful afternoon for my dear wife who ran the show while I kept handy but out of sight. This was a good experience for her. Although she knew that I was available if everything became too much, she managed it all very well.

Afterwards, Margaret was elated - even excited at what she had accomplished. It was a major step forward and one she had longed for. She was back to being a hostess in her own home.

Talk about trial by jury.

Well, in my estimation, that was it and she proved her case admirably.

Naturally, Margaret was tired after everyone had left.

There being no time to think of our evening meal in all the preparations, I had already decided to go down to Victoria and we would have a fish and chip supper.

When I returned, the trays were set, the plates were warming in the oven, the beer glasses were out and the single can of beer with the bottle of lemonade were there to make our shandies.

Almost like old times.

Margaret was profuse with her thanks for my support but I argued that it had all been her own efforts and that I was well-pleased with her personal success.

She went to bed for a well-earned rest after tea and who could blame her. It had been a wonderful day for her.

I remembered about the non-delivery of our microwave oven, but by the time I got through the weekend was upon us and it would have to wait until Monday now.

Was it ever thus?

Well, I was right. There had been a change in Margaret's demeanour. Her performance that day was evidence enough.

In the morning, I overslept a bit. Margaret was up and about and came in with a cup of tea just before eight. Usually on a Saturday, we have made out shopping lists and had breakfast by that time.

I muttered something about the hour going back and we would be alright for time. She countered with the fact that the hour did not go back until early tomorrow morning and did I think today was Sunday?

Now, which one did I say was suffering from brain damage?

We were a bit late going shopping though.

Up until now, I have been the one to say whether Margaret should drive or not according to my perception of her general state of well-being and inclination. Today, without any prompting from me, she just said, 'I'll drive!'

There was now no question in my mind that Friday had been a day of change of season in her illness. The triumph of handling her own tea party had done the trick, or maybe it was just another neurone connection that had come on-line.

The evidence for some critical event was overwhelming. This was a new Margaret.

My own attitude to her development would have to change to avoid future conflict. I would have to quietly retreat a bit into the background of our lives whilst endeavouring to keep constant watch for any relapse, or uncertainty.

This major step forward had to be nurtured in its infancy.

Any sudden trauma could easily reverse the situation and Margaret would lapse back into her world of utter dependence. You can see it happen with children - some of whom never really recover from that first major setback in their individuality, their self-actualisation.

Now it would be a combined operation. Now once again, it would be the two of us against the world.

Chapter Twelve
Grandad will mend it?

It was now some two years since Margaret's accident. If I may say so, it seemed like a lifetime. My wife has improved beyond expectation during this time and bits of her old memory have returned in dribs and drabs.

I firmly believe that Margaret was one of the lucky ones in this respect. The area damaged by her tragic trip and subsequent fall proved in the end to be not too large to prevent a good chance of making a reasonable recovery.

Some people suffer amnesia after a significant blow to the head. Margaret's damage was complicated by the internal bleed and so vital memory banks were destroyed as a result of the tiny injury to some blood vessel within the brain.

In reality, this meant that the old memory banks were now a bit spasmodic in operation on occasion. During conversation, Margaret could often recall people and events clearly, like a record playing a tune once it gets going in the correct groove.

Starting a conversation from scratch was not quite the same. Until the memory was up and running, Margaret would be 'lost'. She needed a cue of some sort to get her on the right track.

After undertaking some research into modern thinking on how the brain operates, I worked my own style of rehabilitation on the following two premises.

Firstly, that the damage to the left side of the brain in a woman need not necessarily mean end of story. Most women use both sides of their brain to think, whereas men tend to use only one side of theirs. The film of '*The Patricia Neal Story*' supported this idea.

(This old B&W film is a 'must see' for all such Carers in my estimation. It helped me to give Margaret the support she needed. It also showed the enormous benefits of having the support of friends and neighbours in the absence of hospital follow-up care).

The second premise was that some of the remaining intact brain cells would be isolated until new connections were made. You could almost feel the change when one of Margaret's synapses snapped into place, or made the connection again.

Whether there was any sense in this approach is outside my understanding. However - just like when the grandchildren break a favourite toy - with Margaret, it was very much of the order of, '*Grandad will find out how to mend it*'.

I am not alone amongst grandads in being familiar with the title phrase of this Chapter in my story. It is par for the course in many families when children break their toys. Applying that same philosophy to my wife Margaret proved to be something different as far as challenges go.

How do you set about mending a broken brain?

Even eminent brain surgeons would have difficulty with that question.

If you are unlucky enough to suffer a head injury, then you need more than just luck to ameliorate the outcome. The area of damage in terms of quantification is one thing. What that area represents as far as function is concerned is quite another.

In Margaret's case, it appears that she has recovered the 90-95% that Dr. Olds, her Geriatrician, predicted. The missing 5-10% is still pretty obvious, though.

She was lucky to be alive. A lot of that luck was due to the fact that she was not taking anti-coagulant drugs such as warfarin when she had the trip and fall. Others that we know about with a similar scenario plus the warfarin, or people undergoing blood anti-coagulant therapy have not been so lucky and have died.

Much of the success of Margaret's recovery was down to her determination to get back the life she discovered she had lived prior to her accident. Without that spark of enthusiasm giving her a daily injection, she would have ended up like many stroke patients – as a perpetual invalid.

If other stroke patients were so motivated, I guess more of them would end up leading useful lives. Yet, despite the possibilities of rehabilitation, once the initial 'medical care' and hospitalised rehabilitation are over, too many stroke patients seem to remain an untrained forgotten burden on their families and friends.

The 'can' is carried by their nearest and dearest if they still have one. This is hardly fair to people who have to give up their own lifestyle because the NHS system cannot, or does not wish to offer post-hospital discharge help to such people.

The ideology of the NHS at inception was a dedicated service from the cradle to the grave. That was how it started when I joined the NHS in September, 1948. Since then, we have acquired administrators. End of story!

My wife and I both paid our taxes and NHS contributions throughout our long working lives, but that counts for nothing, apparently. You should see how much money is owed to the NHS by foreign visitors who take the treatment offered by UK hospitals and then run for cover with no intention of paying. It runs into billions of pounds sterling.

By the way. All the views and comments about the NHS expressed in this book are the personal views of the author. They are based on his personal experience of nearly 40 years working within the NHS. Some of the expensive administrative blunders he is aware of would make your hair curl.

Like the day three pantechnicons rolled up outside St. David's Hospital. The lorries were filled to the brim with toilet rolls.

The Administrative Assistant who ordered them failed to notice that the unit of ordering was 1000. So, for each number he ordered - say 1000 in this case – the supplier sent 1000 of these, or, in essence, 1 million toilet rolls.

Prior to the changes, if something broke in the laboratory, I would ring up the supplier and have a new one delivered. If it was available locally, I would send a van to collect it.

Any patient waiting for pre-op. or post op. test results would have to wait a while if we could not replace the broken equipment immediately.

After the changes, the Supplies Officer used to do the ordering. I would write out a requisition. He would obtain three quotes and post them to me. I would select a supplier and post the quotes back to the Supplies Officer. He would then order the goods.

On one occasion, the three quotes gave him a bit of a problem. One of the quotes said that the firm did not supply the item. Another said that it would take three weeks to obtain the item, since it was not 'in stock'. The third quote said that the item could be supplied from stock immediately and was also the cheapest! What a dilemma for the Supplies Officer to sort out. He had taken the easy option and sent the three quotes to me for my comments.

Meanwhile, the hospital services and the patients suffered. A bed was filled when it could have been emptied. An operation was delayed with the untold consequences for the patient.

The only reason for these adverse comments is because of the effect that the post-1974 administration has had on what was a wonderful organisation of caring, career-trained and qualified, dedicated professional health care staff.

These comments may not be interpreted as applicable to any one specific organisation, hospital or person, but reflect the author's opinion about the effect of the hugely increased administrative presence at the cost of the whole NHS Service.

The lack of NHS support for even one patient can mean that not one life, but several lives suffer. So, in the case of my wife, Margaret, this begs the question of; 'Why is there such a serious gap in the prescribed and expected basic support services in the case of many stroke victims'?

The knock-on effect is that family members who might be contributing to the State economy through their employment tax and other deductions on their remuneration, now become dedicated unpaid home-based family Carers. They should all be entitled to some support if the NHS is for real. If you replace all the administrators with professional staff, we might see some useful changes to the health care scene.

Certainly in our case and in others I have heard of, the Social Services seemed patently unable, or unwilling to cope with the elderly and infirm who are the stroke patients. The fact that such help was written up in Margaret's case-notes indicates that it was prescribed. Therefore, it highlights an administrative gap, or serious fault in the system of health care that no such help ever materialised.

In this instance, as in many such situations when the spouse or other family member is left to pick up the pieces, it may all be down to 'grandad' in the end. My reward for those endeavours is self-evident. With just a few exceptions, my wife is almost once again an 'all-singing, all-dancing' 'best thing since sliced bread' wife once again.

Don't go thinking that this is end of story. This is only the beginning. Overcoming prejudice is one of the biggest problems we have to face. Once normal healthy people hear that someone has had a stroke, they tend to regard that person in a different light. Try treating the stroke patient as a real person and you will have your reward.

Over the ensuing years since the accident, I have continued to support Margaret in all her endeavours. This has enabled her to lead a normal life and enjoy most of the things she did before her accident. Ok, so she can still rely on my support if things go wrong.

I have sent her out into the world with just a mobile phone and a suitcase to attend things such as the Leeds International Piano Competition.

Margaret has always found her way home despite various hang-ups in the travel arrangements.

These trips away from home have given her confidence and enjoyment beyond expectation. On one occasion, she returned to Cardiff from Leeds on a train that was not on any schedule that I could see. That train came into Cardiff Central Station unannounced and just appeared out of the evening gloom, so to speak. As a result, I missed Margaret in the ensuing off-load, so she had a message put over the tannoy for me to meet her at the enquiry desk. How's that for initiative?

Sometimes, Margaret has needed more than a lot of encouragement in order to accomplish her music ambitions. However, the outcomes have justified my backing and my confidence in Margaret's innate ability to succeed.

There have been adequate compensations including her remarkable progress back to more-or-less independence of thought and deed.

In fact – a life again.

John Greenridge, December 2009,

(10th Anniversary of the actual 'Stroke of Misfortune').

www.ingramcontent.com/pod-product-compliance
Lightning Source LLC
Chambersburg PA
CBHW020415290526
45785CB00002B/567